What People Are Saying Abou

"Should be in the library — and kitchen — of every serious cook."
JIM WOOD — Food & Wine Editor — San Francisco Examiner

"A well-organized and user-friendly tribute to many of the state's finest restaurant chefs."
SAN FRANCISCO CHRONICLE

"An attractive guide to the best restaurants and inns, offering recipes from their delectable repertoire of menus."
GAIL RUDDER KENT — Country Inns Magazine

"Outstanding cookbook"
HERITAGE NEWSPAPERS

"I couldn't decide whether to reach for my telephone and make reservations or reach for my apron and start cooking."
JAMES MCNAIR — best-selling cookbook author

"It's an answer to what to eat, where to eat — and how to do it yourself."
THE MONTEREY HERALD

"I dare you to browse through these recipes without being tempted to rush to the kitchen."
PAT GRIFFITH — Chief, Washington Bureau, Blade Communications, Inc.

Books of the "Secrets" Series

The Great Vegetarian Cookbook

The Great California Cookbook

California Wine Country Cooking Secrets

San Francisco's Cooking Secrets

Monterey's Cooking Secrets

New England's Cooking Secrets

Cape Cod's Cooking Secrets

NEW ENGLAND'S COOKING SECRETS

Starring the best restaurants and inns of New England

Kathleen DeVanna Fish

Library of Congress Cataloging-in-Publication Data

NEW ENGLAND'S COOKING SECRETS
Starring the best restaurants and inns of New England

First printing, 1994

Fish, Kathleen DeVanna
94-070384
ISBN 1-883214-02-5
$14.95 softcover
Includes indexes
Autobiography page

Copyright ©1994 by Kathleen DeVanna Fish

Editorial direction by Fred Hernandez
Cover photography by Robert N. Fish
Cover design by Morris Design
Food styling by Susan Devaty
Illustrations by Robin Brickman
Inn sketches by Elna Mira Bjorge – Ultimate Productions
Type by Cimarron Design

Published by Bon Vivant Press
a division of The Marketing Arm
P.O. Box 1994
Monterey, CA 93942

Printed in the United States of America
by Publishers Press

Contents

Prepare To Be Tempted

The bounty of the world's tables came together in New England. Not only were the six states blessed with abundant seafood and game, but the important fishing, shipping and whaling industries brought new people, new ingredients, new methods and new cuisines home to New England. This cookbook/guidebook explores the rich cooking heritage that resulted. We ended up with a fabulous collection of secrets from the finest chefs on the East Coast.

New England's Cooking Secrets features 57 great chefs and 171 kitchen-tested recipes. None of the extraordinary chefs paid to be included in this book. The restaurants and inns were hand-selected and invited to participate.

And since the historically fertile area is so beautiful and attractive to visitors, we included the most notable inns of New England. Line drawings of the inns by our artist will help visitors decide where to stay.

But the bottom line is great food. We concentrated on extraordinary chefs. While you will recognize some of the big names in this book, we have included some who may be new to you. Our requirements were excellence of food, consistency of quality and a flair for beautiful presentation. Some of our chefs cook in large restaurants, some in smaller venues, some in places that the locals would prefer to keep secret.

We took their recipes and adapted them for the home cook. The recipes, presented in an easy-to-use format, complete with cooking times, traverse a wide range of ethnic and culinary tradition. You will discover dishes with origins in Europe, Asia, Africa, Central America, the Caribbean, the Southwest, and indigenous American cuisines. There are vegetarian dishes, seafood, game — and desserts you won't be able to resist.

Some of the recipes are simple. Some are more complex. We stayed clear of purely trendy food, preferring to stress foods that we know to be perfectly delicious. To make things easy, we list the recipes in these categories: Breakfast, Appetizers, Breads, Soups, Salads and Dressings, Main Courses, Vegetables and Side Dishes, Seafood, Poultry, Game, Meat, Sauces and Condiments and Final Temptations.

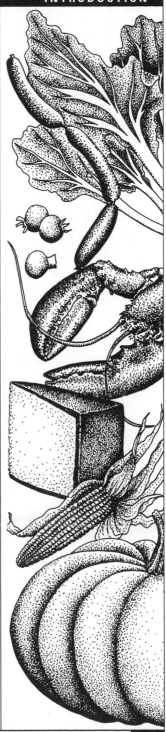

Because New England is so rich in history, natural beauty and tradition, it is an enormous draw to visitors. We decided to do some exploring in order to provide some historical perspective. State by state, we offer historical highlights, local lore and tips every visitor should know. We added historic photos that will help you put it all together.

While researching New England, we came across many fascinating tidbits you won't find anywhere else. For example, we discovered a Wedding Cake House whose original owner was a sea captain. Because he had to set sail in the middle of his wedding, he ordered the carpenters to complete the ornate house as a consolation prize for his bride.

We also found out the origins of Naugahyde. And we talk about a huge store that boasts six parking lots and a trout pond inside the men's department. In fact, some shoppers will want to know where the best factory outlets are located. We point out some of the best locations.

We'll tell you about a town that decided to attract visitors by building sidewalks made of marble — 17 miles of marble. We'll also tell you where to find a cemetery that features a granite armchair and statues of a husband and wife sitting up in bed.

You'll learn about lots of famous people, including General Tom Thumb, Mark Twain, Noah Webster, Presidents George Bush, Calvin Coolidge and Franklin D. Roosevelt, Christopher Columbus, Winslow Homer, Robert Frost, Ethan Allen, Leif Ericson and Ben and Jerry of ice cream fame.

Included are stories about Yankee peddlers, Norsemen, Shakers, Clydesdale horses, and where the first rays of the morning sun hit the U.S. mainland.

We'll also discuss pirate treasure, why the first presidential election returns always come from Dixville Notch, and which state has no earned-income tax or retail sales tax. We'll also tell you where to find a 10-foot statue of Buddha, a replica of the famed grotto at Lourdes, and where to find the country's most-climbed mountain.

It's all in New England.

The rich American tapestry of history and cuisine owes much to New England. Explore with us and you will learn a lot. But more importantly, your cooking skills and palate will become richer. Let us show you how.

New England States

MAINE

Bangor

Blue Hill

Augusta   Camden   Bar Harbor

VERMONT

Burlington

Middlebury   Jackson
                    Tamworth
Brandon   Orford

Woodstock

Portland

NEW
HAMPSHIRE   Kennebunkport

Bennington   Manchester   Portsmouth

Williamstown

Salem

Northampton   Cambridge   Boston

MASSACHUSETTS   Provincetown

Springfield

Manchester   Providence

Hartford

CONNECTICUT   Martha's Vineyard

Danbury   Newport   Nantucket

New Haven   Block   RHODE
                   Island   ISLAND

New England Restaurants and Inns

Connecticut Restaurants

Connecticut Inns

Rhode Island Restaurants

Rhode Island Inns

Massachusetts Restaurants

Cape Cod, Martha's Vineyard & Nantucket Restaurants

Massachusetts Inns

Vermont Restaurants

Vermont Inns

New Hampshire Restaurants

New Hampshire Inns

Maine Restaurants

Maine Inns

Chefs' Favorite Recipes

Breakfast

German Coffeecake—**Hartstone Inn**, *271*

Strawberry Mascarpone Filled Crêpes—**Lambert's Cove Country Inn**, *171*

Baked Eggs—**Hartstone Inn**, *272*

West Mountain Eggs with Béarnaise Sauce—**West Mountain Inn**, *207*

Poached Pears with Raspberry Sauce—**Hartstone Inn**, *273*

Salmon Hash with Poached Eggs—**The White Hart**, *41*

French Toast—**White Goose Inn**, *235*

Appetizers

Maine Crabcakes—**Christian's**, *141*

Crab Claws with Celery Root Remoulade—**Butler's**, *179*

Lobster Madeira Crêpes—**The Inn at Mystic**, *49*

Oyster and Spinach Custard, Saffron Beurre Blanc—**L'Etoile**, *153*

Cassoulet d'Escargot—**The Homestead Inn**, *45*

Foie Gras with Mango and Raspberries—**L'Etoile**, *154*

Lobster and Corn Fritters—**Arrows**, *242*

Roasted Oysters—**Olives**, *123*

Pâté Maison—**Pot au Feu**, *65*

Salmon Gravlax with Tarragon Mustard Horseradish Sauce—**Warriners**, *157*

Mousseline of Three Salmon—**The Prince & The Pauper**, *197*

Grilled Quail with Ham and Cucumber Salad—**Christmas Farm Inn**, *229*

Stir-Fry Mussels—**The Belmont**, *267*

Angel Hair Pasta with Smoked Trout—**Tollgate Hill**, *51*

Salads and Dressings

Vegetables & Side Dishes

Main Courses

Seafood

Poultry

Game

Meat

Sauces & Condiments

Final Temptations

New England's Cooking Stars

ADESSO
Menu for Four   **56**

CHICKEN BREAST SALAD
IN CHAMPAGNE VINAIGRETTE
BLACK PEPPER LINGUINE IN PINK VODKA SAUCE
GRILLED PORK CHOPS IN HONEY GINGER

ARROWS
Menu for Four   **240**

SZECHUAN CABBAGE SALAD
LOBSTER & CORN FRITTERS
PAPAYA CARROT SALAD
RISOTTO WITH TOMATOES & SWISS CHARD

THE BACK BAY GRILL
Menu for Six   **246**

GRILLED PORTOBELLOS WITH ONION MARMALADE
NUT CRUSTED TROUT WITH MUSTARD CREAM
BLACKBERRY & RASPBERRY GRATIN

THE BELMONT
Menu for Six   **250**

SHRIMP SOUP
LOBSTER PAD THAI
APPLE CRANBERRY CROSTATA

BLUE STRAWBERRY
Menu for Eight   **214**

CURRY TOMATO CREAM SOUP
GREENS WITH SWEET & SOUR RASPBERRY
ROASTED DUCK ON RED PEPPER PURÉE
ROASTED LEG OF LAMB IN MINT

BUTLER'S
Menu for Four   **178**

CRAB CLAWS WITH CELERY ROOT REMOULADE
VEGETABLES IN SMOKED TOMATO ALE SAUCE
HICKORY SMOKED SALMON WITH WILD RICE
FROZEN MARGARITA PARFAIT

CAFÉ ALWAYS

Menu for Four   **254**

OYSTERS WITH CHAMPAGNE & PINK PEPPERCORN

LOBSTER WITH THAI COCONUT CURRY SAUCE

LEMON PUDDING CAKE

CAFÉ DÉJÀ VU

Menu for Four   **186**

CRABCAKES WITH MUSTARD CAPER SAUCE

SWEET POTATO SALAD

CRANBERRY GINGER SCALLOPS

THE CASTINE INN

Menu for Four   **258**

BAKED EGGPLANT & TOMATO SALAD

CRABMEAT CAKES WITH MUSTARD SAUCE

BLUEBERRY PIE

THE CHANTICLEER

Menu for Four   **132**

CREAM OF ASPARAGUS SOUP

CHICKEN STUFFED WITH HERBS

CHOCOLATE DECADENCE WITH ESPRESSO SAUCE

CHILLINGSWORTH

Menu for Four   **136**

OYSTERS & SPINACH IN PUFF PASTRY

TWO MELON SOUP WITH CHAMPAGNE & MINT

LOBSTER WITH SPINACH IN COGNAC CREAM

CHRISTIAN'S

Menu for Eight   **140**

ROAST DUCK WITH PEAR AVOCADO SAUCE
COCONUT RUM CARAMEL CUSTARD
WITH ROASTED BANANA SAUCE

DALI

Menu for Six   **86**

COLD ALMOND AND CUCUMBER SOUP
GARDEN PAELLA
CARAMELIZED BABY EGGPLANT

DAN'L WEBSTER INN

Menu for Four   **144**

SMOKED DUCKLING SALAD
MACADAMIA & CASHEW CRUSTED BASS
PINEAPPLE MASCARPONE VELVET

D'ARTAGNAN

Menu for Eight   **220**

SALAD OF VENISON IN WALNUT VINAIGRETTE
ROAST RABBIT WITH MUSTARD SAUCE
PEAR ALMOND CREAM TART

EAST COAST GRILL

Menu for Four   **90**

TANGERINE GLAZED GRILLED SHRIMP SKEWER
JAVA SALAD
DRIED FRUIT & APPLE SALAD
STUFFED QUAIL WITH BRUSSELS SPROUTS
PUMPKIN BREAD PUDDING

FINE BOUCHE

Menu for Eight   **30**

SALMON WITH TANGERINE SALSA
WILD MUSHROOM RAVIOLI
DUCK BREASTS WITH BLUEBERRIES & CASSIS

FLOOD TIDE RESTAURANT

Menu for Six   **34**

CAESAR SALAD
BEEF WELLINGTON
BANANAS FOSTER

HAMMERSLEY'S BISTRO

Menu for Six   **96**

VEAL STEW WITH TARRAGON
TUNA IN SUN-DRIED TOMATO COMPOTE
BROWN BUTTER & ALMOND TART

THE HARVEST

Menu for Four   **100**

BRAISED RABBIT WITH PAPPARDELLE NOODLES
STUFFED RACK OF LAMB
ROASTED MONKFISH IN SAMBUCA CREAM BROTH

JASPER'S

Menu for Four   **104**

OYSTER STEW
HALF-CRISPY FISH WITH SCALLION PURÉE
PEAR UPSIDE-DOWN SPICE CAKE

JONATHAN'S

Menu for Six **262**

WARM SALAD WITH SMOKED MUSSELS & CHEVRE
DRUNKEN RABBIT WITH MAPLE BARBECUE SAUCE
SOUTHERN COMFORT RAISIN BREAD PUDDING

JULIEN

Menu for Four **108**

LOBSTER SOUFFLÉ
SEAFOOD POT AU FEU
MUSHROOMS IN PUFF PASTRY SHELLS

L'ESPALIER

Menu for Six **112**

CHANTERELLE CAPPUCCINO SOUP
PECAN CRUSTED SPRING LAMB
BLOOD ORANGE SOUFFLÉ

LAMBERT'S COVE COUNTRY INN

Menu for Four **148**

SHRIMP, SCALLOPS & ANDOUILLE SAUSAGE STEW
GRILLED SWORDFISH WITH
MANGOS & SWEET PEPPERS
VANILLA MOUSSE

L'ETOILE

Menu for Four **152**

OYSTER & SPINACH CUSTARD
FOIE GRAS
WHITE CHOCOLATE RASPBERRY TART

MICHELA'S

Menu for Four   **116**

ROASTED PEAR RADICCHIO SALAD
BRODETTO OF BASS WITH TOMATOES
SEARED QUAIL ON POLENTA

MIDDLEBROOK RESTAURANT

Menu for Six   **192**

SALMON & ASPARAGUS CHOWDER
CHEDDAR & DILL BISCUITS
GREENS IN CHIVE BLOSSOM DIJON VINAIGRETTE

OLIVES

Menu for Six   **122**

ROASTED OYSTERS
RED PEPPER SALAD
MARINATED LAMB SANDWICH

THE PLACE AT YESTERDAY'S

Menu for Four   **60**

SWEET POTATO BISQUE
HALIBUT IN A CURRY CRUST
CRANBERRY BREAD PUDDING

POT AU FEU

Menu for Four   **64**

PATÉ MAISON
FRENCH ONION SOUP
GREENS WITH GOAT CHEESE
POT AU FEU
CREME BRULÉE

THE PRINCE & THE PAUPER

Menu for Four   **196**

MOUSSELINE OF THREE SALMON
ASPARAGUS VICHYSSOISE
ROAST CHICKEN WITH MORELS
BOURBON PECAN CHEESECAKE

SCOTTISH LION INN

Menu for Six   **224**

TOMATO CHEDDAR SOUP

BRUNSWICK STEW

KONA COFFEE FREEZE

SEASONS

Menu for Six   **128**

ROASTED PUMPKIN SOUP

CHARRED SQUID & ASPARAGUS SALAD

TROUT WITH BRAISED OLIVES

WARRINERS

Menu for Eight   **156**

SALMON GRAVLAX WITH
TARRAGON MUSTARD HORSERADISH SAUCE

SAUTÉED SCALLOPS

THE WHITE HART

Menu for Six   **38**

ROASTED TOMATO SOUP WITH BASIL PURÉE

GOAT CHEESE DUMPLINGS

SALMON HASH WITH POACHED EGGS

THE WHITE HORSE TAVERN

Menu for Four   **70**

GRILLED SUMMER BISQUE

VEAL TENDERLOIN IN POTATO NEST

TRIPLE SILK

THE WOODBOX

Menu for Four   **160**

SMOKED SALMON QUESADILLA

MEDALLIONS OF VENISON

CHOCOLATE BOURBON PECAN CAKE

CONNECTICUT: The Clever Yankee Spirit

Connecticut, the southernmost state in New England, is known to many people as the epitome of American know-how. Mark Twain, one of the state's best known inhabitants, even named his inventive traveler "The Connecticut Yankee in King Arthur's Court." And there were many other clever characters from Connecticut: inventor Eli Whitney, clockmaker Seth Thomas, and Sameul Colt, who invented the revolver.

But perhaps the craftiest Connecticut resident of them all was circus showman Phineas T. Barnum, who lived in Bridgeport. In fact, Barnum's most famous attraction, Tom Thumb, who measured only 28 inches in height, also was a citizen of the state.

Connecticut Yankee peddlers were among the first to take advantage of the state's technology geared to precision parts. The peddlers loaded their wagons with the buttons, pins, kitchenwares and interchangeable small parts manufactured in Connecticut and traveled from door to door — and eventualy West with the settlers — selling their goods.

The state's first nickname — "The Nutmeg State" — derived from these peddlers, many of whom sold nutmeg. But much of their nutmeg turned out to be fake, so the nickname later was changed to "The Constitution State" in honor of the Fundamental Orders of Connecticut, a 1639 document cited as a forerunner of the United States Constitution.

The state was first established with three 17th century settlements. In 1633, a group from the Plymouth Colony sailed up the Connecticut River (called Quinnehtukqut, or "long tidal river" by the Indians) and established a colony at Windsor. They were soon followed by settlers who founded Wethersfield and Hartford (now the state capital).

The settlers had been looking for fertile land and Connecticut did not disappoint them.

Crops of tobacco, corn, grain and vegetables were plentiful. But soon, industry and manufacturing were established. The resultant textile mills, copper mines and ironworks drew more and more residents and today the state is densely populated.

But the clever Yankee spirit is still alive today in Connecticut — in the manufacture of brassware, hardware, fine silver, helicopters, atomic submarines and rubber tires and goods. In fact, here's a bit of Connecticut trivia that will

★

*Two Victorian women enjoy tea,
circa 1890.*

*P.T. Barnum in an 1850 engraving by
John Chester Buttre.*

trip up many opponents: Where does Naugahyde come from? From Naugatuck, Conn., where the synthetic leather is made.

Connecticut has many claims to fame. With over four dozen insurance firms based in Hartford, it has become the insurance capital of America. The state was home to writers Mark Twain and Harriet Beecher Stowe, and lexicographer Noah Webster.

The state is home to prestigious Yale University, the submarine capital of the world (Groton and New London), Mystic Seaport (the "living" museum of 19th century New England maritime life), and even an actor's home (Gillette Castle) that was turned into a state park.

Here are some of the highlights of a visit to Connecticut:

HARTFORD — Bushnell Park is home to the State Capitol, which boasts a golden dome surrounded by 12 pillars. Also in Bushnell Park, ride the 48 hand-carved horses of the restored 1914 carousel while listening to the 1925 Wurlitzer band organ. Nearby is the Wadsworth Atheneum, said to be the first public art museum in America. Close to downtown Hartford is Nook Farm, which includes the homes of Mark Twain and Harriet Beecher Stowe. Aircraft fans may want to visit the New England Air Museum at Bradley International Airport. Over 75 aircraft are on display, as is a jet fighter cockpit simulator. And in West Hartford, you'll find the Noah Webster House and Museum.

NEW HAVEN — Home of Yale University, which was founded in 1701, but was moved to New Haven in 1716. The campus features Harkness Tower, with its famous motto: "For God, for country, and for Yale." Other Yale attractions are the Yale Art Gallery (oldest college art museum in the country), the Peabody Museum of Natural History (largest of its kind in New England), and the Yale Collection of Musical Instruments (over 800 instruments, some dating to the 16th century).

BRIDGEPORT — The home of P.T. Barnum (who once was mayor) and tiny Tom Thumb, Bridgeport is the site of the Barnum Museum. Features include Barnum's personal belongings and memorabilia of Thumb and Jenny Lind, the "Swedish Nightingale." Other attractions: a scaled-down version of Barnum's three-ring circus and a wooden replica of a Swiss village. A life-size statue of Tom Thumb stands in downtown Bridgeport.

NEW LONDON/GROTON — You can visit the U.S. Coast Guard Academy in New London. If its training barque "Eagle" is in port, you can go aboard on weekends. Across the Thames River (rhymes with James) is the United States Naval Submarine Base, headquarters for the North Atlantic Fleet. The world's first nuclear submarine, the USS Nautilus, is permanently berthed here. Look for the lavish homes of wealthy sea captains along the river and oceanfront. And if you want to see more of the sea, take a cruise on Project Oceanology's *Enviro-Lab,* a 55-foot oceanographic research vessel.

MYSTIC — Here's a chance to sample the life of the early New England seafarer. This re-created "living" museum, comprising 17 acres, is the country's biggest maritime museum. Features include the "Charles W. Morgan," last of the wooden whaling ships, shops where you'll find coopers, blacksmiths, sail makers, wood carvers and candlemakers. Steamboat cruises also are available, and you can visit taverns, general stores, a schoolhouse, a bank, a chapel and historic homes. Kids enjoy the Children's Museum, where they can dress in 19th-century clothing. ✫

Picnickers enjoy lunch near Mystic, Connecticut, circa 1900.

Photos from the Connecticut Historical Society.

FINE BOUCHE

FRENCH CUISINE
78 Main Street
Centerbrook, Connecticut
(203) 767-1277
Dinner Tuesday–Sunday 5:30PM–9PM
AVERAGE DINNER FOR TWO: $80

Set in a Victorian mansion in the Centerbrook region of Essex, Fine Bouche offers elegant French dining with an exceptional wine list — over 450 wines from around the world. The finest china glitters in candlelight, highlighting the sumptuous food. Diners are expected to enjoy their evening, and with the help of the expert staff, need not be connoisseurs.

Chef/owner Steve Wilkinson is poetic and romantic about his food. He once gave a series of dinners based on the Academy Award-winning Danish film, "Babette's Feast." The elaborate meal featured Buckwheat Crêpes with Crème Fraîche and Caviar, and Roast Quail stuffed with fresh Truffles and Foie Gras served in a Puff Pastry Shell.

Samples from the current menu include a Phyllo Purse with Crab, Black Bean Salsa and Lime Cilantro Dressing; Pear, Goat Cheese and Prosciutto on Endive with Walnuts and Raspberry Vinegar; Pork Noisettes sautéed with Apples, Cream and Apple Brandy; Duck Breasts sautéed with a Green Peppercorn Sauce and Tournedos of Beef in Madeira and Truffle Sauce.

FINE BOUCHE'S MENU FOR EIGHT

Salmon with Tangerine Salsa and Lime Beurre Blanc

Wild Mushroom Ravioli

Duck Breasts with Blueberries and Cassis

Salmon with Tangerine Salsa and Lime Beurre Blanc

L ightly grate the outer tangerine rind. Peel the remaining pith, then chop, removing the membranes and seeds.

Mix the tangerine, cumin, chile sauce, red pepper, onion, papaya or mango, honey and chopped cilantro in a mixing bowl. Let stand. This keeps well in the refrigerator.

In a small saucepan, reduce the wine and shallot by half. Add the cream and reduce by half. Season to taste. Whisk in ½ cup (1 stick) butter in pieces. Grate the outer lime rinds into the sauce. Add the lime juice to taste. Adjust the seasonings if desired.

Slice the salmon into 2 oz. portions at a 45° angle. Sprinkle with salt and pepper, then dot with remaining butter.

Broil until firm, but do not overcook.

Place the salmon in the center of individual plates. Spoon sauces on either side. Garnish with cilantro leaves.

Trade Secret: A substitute for the Thai chile sauce is ½ tsp. hot pepper flakes with 1 Tbsp. orange marmalade.

Serves 8
Preparation Time:
  30 Minutes

  4 tangerines
 ½ tsp. cumin powder
  1 Tbsp. Thai sweet chile sauce
 ½ sweet red pepper, seeded, chopped
 ½ small red onion, chopped
 ½ papaya or mango, seeded, chopped
 ¼ cup honey
 ¼ cup fresh cilantro, chopped
 ½ cup dry white wine
  1 shallot, finely chopped
  2 cups heavy cream
    Salt and white pepper to taste
 ¾ cup (1½ sticks) butter
  3 limes
  1 Salmon filet, 1 lb.
    Cilantro leaves for garnish

★

Wild Mushroom Ravioli

Serves 8
Preparation Time:
  30 Minutes

  1 lb. ravioli, about 30
     pieces
  1 cup olive oil
  1 lb. large oyster
     mushrooms
  2 garlic cloves
  1 sprig fresh rosemary
     Kosher salt and pepper
     to taste
  1 cup dry white wine
  8 oz. goat cheese
     Rosemary for garnish

C ook the ravioli in boiling salted water. Rinse in cold water and drain. Toss with ½ cup olive oil.

Cut the stems off the mushrooms.

Chop the garlic and rosemary leaves. Mix with the remaining olive oil, salt and pepper. Toss the mushrooms in the oil mixture and place on the grill until done, about 3 to 5 minutes, being careful to turn mushrooms and not to let oil ignite.

Pour the wine into a shallow baking dish. Arrange the ravioli, leaving space in the center for mushrooms. Place pieces of goat cheese around the ravioli. Cover and place in a warm oven until the cheese melts.

Place the mushrooms in the center of the dish and garnish with sprigs of rosemary.

Duck Breasts with Blueberries and Cassis

eat the sugar and water in a small covered saucepan until dissolved. Remove the lid and cook until dark, but do not burn.

Remove the pan from the heat and add the vinegar carefully; it will bubble.

Add the wine and veal stock; simmer until reduced by half. Add the Cassis to taste.

Score the skin of the duck breasts; do not cut through to the meat. Season to taste.

Pre-heat a large, heavy skillet, then cook the duck breasts skin side down, skimming off the fat as needed until brown. Turn and cook on the meat side until medium-rare, about 2 minutes. Cool, then slice the duck breasts.

Add the blueberries to the warm sauce, then stir in the butter.

Arrange the duck breasts in a fan shape on plates. Spoon the sauce over the meat.

Serves 8
Preparation Time:
  30 Minutes

  ½ **cup sugar**
  ½ **cup water**
  ½ **cup red wine vinegar**
  1 **cup red wine**
  4 **cups veal stock**
  ¾ **cup Crème de Cassis**
  4 **duck breasts, boned**
    Kosher salt and pepper
    to taste
  2 **cups blueberries**
  4 **Tbsps. butter**

THE FLOOD TIDE RESTAURANT

CONTINENTAL CUISINE
Jct. Routes 1 and 27
Mystic, Connecticut
(203) 536-8140
Breakfast, Lunch and Dinner 7AM–10PM
AVERAGE DINNER FOR TWO: $50

T he Flood Tide's elegance and atmosphere are unmatched in this area. Located at The Inn at Mystic, the restaurant is perched atop a hill overlooking romantic Mystic Harbor. This is the place to celebrate a special occasion. Live piano music floats softly over crisp, white woodwork, abundant fresh flower arrangements, and mirrors behind greenery filled with sparkling white lights. Chandeliers in every room flatter the white linens and sparkling, pink-stemmed crystal.

The service, food and atmosphere are all five-star. Variety and presentation draw attention to every dish on the menu. Dinner possibilities include a Brie and Leek Soufflé, Roasted Pheasant, Rainbow Trout with Toasted Nuts and Amaretto Cream, Broiled Scallops with a Fresh Basil Crust and Filet Mignon with Mushrooms.

The extensive dessert menu tops off the dinners with such delights as Fruited Ice Cream Tulip, Gingered Creme Caramel, Raspberry Kiwi Parfait, and the flaming Strawberries Romanoff.

THE FLOOD TIDE RESTAURANT'S MENU FOR SIX

Caesar Salad

Beef Wellington

Bananas Foster

Caesar Salad

I n a large salad bowl, combine the pepper and anchovy. Mix thoroughly with a fork, making a paste. Add the garlic, mixing in the same way. Squeeze in the lemon juice, then add the egg yolks and blend.

While stirring, add the oil in a stream until the dressing reaches the right consistency — smooth, yellow, and clinging to the sides of the bowl.

Add the croutons and lettuce and toss until the lettuce is coated. Sprinkle with the cheese and toss again. Serve immediately.

Serves 6
Preparation Time:
  10 Minutes

1½ Tbsps. pepper
½ Tbsp. anchovy filets, minced
3 to 4 large garlic cloves, pressed or finely chopped
  Juice of 1½ lemons
3 egg yolks
3 cups olive oil
¾ cup croutons
2 heads Romaine lettuce, washed, cut into medium pieces
  Parmesan cheese to taste

☆

Beef Wellington

Serves 6
Preparation Time:
  30 Minutes
Cooking Time:
  30 Minutes

  3 **beef tenderloins, 1 lb.**
     each, trimmed
  3 **lbs. ground pork**
  ¾ **lb. duck livers**
  3 **bay leaves**
  3 **tsps. thyme**
  3 **tsps. sage**
     Pepper to taste
  ¾ **cup brandy**
  ¾ **cup Worcestershire**
     sauce
  3 **puff pastry sheets,**
     10"×15"
  3 **eggs, beaten**

I n a hot skillet, sear the tenderloins on all sides. Cool and set aside.
   In a large skillet combine the pork, duck livers, bay leaves, thyme, sage and pepper. Cook until well done.

Place mixture in a food processor and purée until very smooth to a pâté-like consistency. Add the brandy and Worcestershire sauce. Cool.

Spread the pâté on one side of the tenderloins. Place tenderloin, paté side down, in the center of a pastry sheet and wrap, making sure all sides are tightly sealed.

Place on a greased sheet pan, seam sides down, and brush the top with the beaten eggs.

Bake at 400° until desired doneness, about 30 minutes for medium.

Bananas Foster

Melt the butter in a pan. Stir in the brown sugar and cook until the sugar starts to caramelize.

Add the orange juice and liqueur, mixing well. Add the walnuts and bananas and sprinkle with cinnamon. Flame with rum.

Serve over ice cream.

Serves 6
Preparation Time:
  15 Minutes

  ¼ cup (½ stick) butter
  6 Tbsps. brown sugar
    Juice of 1½ oranges
  ½ cup Creme de Banana
    liqueur
  3 Tbsps. walnuts,
    chopped
  5 bananas, sliced
    Ground cinnamon
    Rum
    Ice Cream

★

THE WHITE HART

AMERICAN CUISINE
The Village Green
Salisbury, Connecticut
(203) 435-0030
Breakfast Monday–Saturday 7:30AM–10AM
Brunch Sunday 7:30AM–12PM
Lunch Daily 11:30AM–2:30PM
Dinner Sunday–Thursday 5PM–9:30PM
        Friday–Saturday 5PM–10:30PM
AVERAGE DINNER FOR TWO: $50

A Salisbury landmark, the gracious White Hart inn hosts three restaurants: the light, airy Garden Room with its glass walls, the elegant Sea Grill and the more relaxed Tap Room. All feature exquisite, highly-rated food, and the Sea Grill specializes in tantalizingly prepared shellfish. The restaurants are loyally patronized by local citizens. The Colonial decor and soft touches of the inn pervade the restaurants as well, offering diners a classic country inn experience. The Tap Room is like an old tavern, with warm woods and tables dating back to the old days of the inn.

Menu selections include Three Bean Chili, Roasted Sweet Potato Soup with Crème Fraîche and Smoked Scallops, Grilled Rosemary Shrimp over Polenta, Grilled Zucchini Lasagna, Pan Seared Tuna with Soy Ginger Beurre Blanc, and Grilled Breast of Chicken with Ragout of Artichoke.

THE WHITE HART'S MENU FOR SIX

Roasted Tomato Soup with Basil Purée

Goat Cheese Dumplings

Salmon Hash with Poached Eggs

Roasted Tomato Soup with Basil Purée

C ore the tomatoes and place them on a sheet pan with the hole facing up. Sprinkle garlic and thyme on top and drizzle ½ cup olive oil over the tomatoes.

Roast the tomatoes in the oven at 350° until very soft, about 45 minutes. Remove the tomatoes from the oven and allow to cool.

In a medium stock pot, sauté the onions in ½ cup olive oil over medium heat until translucent. Add the tomatoes and half of the basil. Sauté for 15 minutes. Add the chicken stock. Continue to simmer for 30 minutes. Remove from heat and cool.

Pass through a medium food mill, or purée and pass through a coarse strainer. Return the soup to heat. Season to taste.

Purée the remaining basil in a food processor. Drizzle the remaining oil into the basil. Season to taste.

Ladle soup into bowls. Drizzle purée over the soup. Scoop out dumplings with a small scoop and place in the center of the bowl. Garnish with a sprig of basil.

Serves 6
Preparation Time:
  20 Minutes
Cooking Time:
  1 Hour, 30 Minutes

  6 lbs. tomatoes
 12 garlic cloves, finely
    chopped
 12 thyme sprigs, leaves
    chopped
1½ cups olive oil
  2 large onions, medium
    diced
  1 bunch basil, leaves
    removed
  1 qt. chicken stock
    Salt and pepper to
    taste
    Goat cheese
    dumplings, optional
    (recipe follows)

Goat Cheese Dumplings

Serves 6
Preparation Time:
  10 Minutes
Cooking Time:
  30 Minutes

  1 lb. potatoes, peeled
  1 Tbsp. salt
  1 lb. goat cheese

Quarter each potato and put them in a pot. Cover with cold water and salt. Bring potatoes to a boil. Lower heat and simmer until potatoes can be easily pierced with a fork.

Remove from heat and rinse in cold water. When potatoes are cool, pass them through a fine food mill, or coarsely process in a food processor.

Fold in the goat cheese until well mixed. Season to taste.

Scoop out dumplings with a small scoop and serve in soup.

Salmon Hash with Poached Eggs

Sauté the potatoes in butter in small amounts until golden brown and slightly crispy. Remove from heat and reserve.

Bring 2 qts. water with vinegar and 1 Tbsp. salt to a boil for poaching eggs.

Add eggs to the poaching water. Remove at desired doneness.

Sauté all the peppers and onion until they begin to turn transparent. Add the potatoes and season well with salt and pepper. Cook until well heated. Divide onto each plate.

Quickly grill the salmon enough to heat through. Place in the center of the potatoes on each plate.

Place two eggs on each plate and garnish with chopped chives.

Trade Secret: At The White Hart, this dish is served with a beurre blanc or hollandaise sauce.

Serves 4
Preparation Time:
  30 Minutes

4 to 5 medium potatoes, diced ³⁄₈″
  Butter for sautéing
1 Tbsp. salt
2 Tbsps. distilled vinegar
8 eggs
1 small red bell pepper, finely diced
1 small yellow bell pepper, finely diced
1 small green bell pepper, finely diced
1 small onion, finely diced
  Salt and pepper to taste
4 salmon pieces, 3 to 4 oz. each, sliced ⅛″ thick
  Chives, slices ¼″ for garnish

★

THE BOULDERS

Route 45, East Shore Road
New Preston, Connecticut 06777
(203) 868-0541
ROOM RATES: $175–$265
AMENITIES: Seventeen rooms, including two suites, with private baths, many with fire-places. Breakfast is included. Lake views, private decks and terraces. Activities offered: swimming, bicycling, boating, fishing, tennis, golf, horseback riding. Located near antique and craft shops, summer theater and music festivals; and, in the winter, cross-country and down-hill skiing.
DIRECTIONS: Take Hwy. 8 to Route 202 at Torrington. Take Route 202 west to Route 45 in New Preston. Take Route 45 north to The Boulders on the left.

T he Boulders is a retreat with stunning lake and mountain views, graciously decorated rooms with antiques, fireplaces and terraces in the main house, guest houses and the carriage house. The main house is a stone and shingle estate built as a family home in 1895. Owners Kees and Ulla Adema have decorated with American folk art, wood and brass beds, hundred-year-old quilts, and marble-top tables. The warm woods of the house surround the stone fireplaces for a warm, cozy atmosphere in real luxury. The inn is an idyllic setting for weddings or executive retreats, with services available for both.

The restaurant is renowned for fine dining. In either the dining room or on the terrace, the views and the fare are spectacular. Chef William F. Okesson is impeccably trained and serves such examples of New American cuisine as Quail with Fresh Morels and Cream, Roast Duck with Grand Marnier, Grilled Swordfish or Tenderloins Stuffed with Spinach, Tomatoes and Pine Nuts.

Lobster with Sweet Potato Gnocchi and Vanilla Butter Sauce

Steam the potatoes and peel. Mash or put through a potato ricer.

Put 1¾ cups flour in a mixing bowl. Mix in potatoes. Add the eggs and nutmeg and season to taste. If dough is too sticky, add more flour.

On a floured table, divide dough into quarters. Roll out into long ropes and cut into 1" lengths. The gnocchi can be made ahead of time and refrigerated.

Put the lobsters in a pot and cover with cold water. Add the lemon juice. Bring the water just to a boil on high heat. Turn off the heat and allow to set for about 10 minutes. Remove and clean the lobsters, removing all claw and tail meat. Keep the meat warm.

Heat a saucepan with a small amount of butter and sweat the shallots without browning. When soft, add the wine, vinegar, vanilla bean and sugar. Cook on high heat until reduced to a syrup. Do not brown. Add the cream and reduce by half. Slowly whisk in the butter, removing the pan from the heat occasionally. Strain the sauce through a fine mesh strainer.

Bring a pot of salted water to a boil. Add the gnocchi. When they float to the top, boil one minute more and remove. Place in a sauté pan with melted butter, salt and pepper over medium heat until lightly browned. Remove gnocchi and place spinach in the same pan. Wilt spinach and season to taste.

Divide the spinach onto 4 plates, making nests. Place gnocchi on the spinach. Pour the sauce around the nests. Place the warm lobster around the nests, cutting the tails into fourths. Garnish with chervil sprigs and serve immediately.

Serves 4
Preparation Time:
  1 Hour, 30 Minutes

  1 lb. sweet potatoes
  2 cups flour, unbleached
  2 eggs
  ⅛ tsp. nutmeg
    Salt and pepper to
    taste
  4 lobsters
    Juice of 2 lemons
  1 lb. butter, cubed
  2 shallots, peeled, thinly
    sliced
  1 cup white wine
  ¼ cup white wine
    vinegar
  ½ vanilla bean, split
  1 Tbsp. sugar
  2 Tbsps. heavy cream
  1 lb. spinach, stemmed,
    washed
    Chervil sprigs for
    garnish

THE HOMESTEAD INN

420 Field Point Road
Greenwich, Connecticut 06830
(203) 869-7500
ROOM RATES: $92–$185
AMENITIES: Seventeen rooms and 6 suites in three buildings, with private baths, private porches, full-service French restaurant, continental breakfast, meeting facilities, landscaped gardens and grounds. Convenient access to New York City.
DIRECTIONS: Take I-95 to Exit 3 and turn west onto Arch Street in Greenwich. Turn left at the Horseneck Lane light. At the end of Horseneck Lane, turn left onto Field Point Road. The inn is ¼ mile on the right.

T he Homestead Inn exudes elegance. Owners Lessie Davison and Nancy Smith say it has "opulence with a down-home flavor." The main building dates from 1799, and was impeccably restored to its current beauty in 1979. The rooms feature refined antiques and comfortable country furnishings. The Cottage is a meeting facility for up to 25, and has a smaller room for up to 12.

La Grange Restaurant provides classic French fare, under the leadership of Chef Jacques Thiebeult, formerly of LeCirque in New York City. The dining room and porch of La Grange show their origins as an old barn which was grafted onto the house. The decor of the restaurant features posts and beams, iron chandeliers and other colonial touches; the porch wraps around a corner, providing expansive views of the grounds.

The menu often features seasonal dishes with local game, as well as delicacies like Duck Terrine with Pistachios and Truffles, or Sweetbreads in Madeira.

Cassoulet d'Escargot

Sauté snails and chanterelles in 1 Tbsp. butter with shallots. Add the remaining butter and garlic. Let melt and stir lightly. Add the cream and Pernod. Let mixture reduce somewhat.

Sprinkle with chopped parsley and serve immediately.

Serves 4
Preparation Time:
   15 Minutes

24 snails
½ cup chanterelle
   mushrooms
5 Tbsps. butter
2 tsps. shallots, chopped
2 garlic cloves, minced
½ cup heavy cream
½ tsp. Pernod, optional
   Parsley, chopped

Grilled Swordfish with Citrus Vinaigrette

Serves 4
Preparation Time:
  20 Minutes

- ¾ cup sherry vinegar
- 2 cups olive oil
- ½ tsp. five-spice powder
- 2 Tbsps. soy sauce
- 2 Tbsps. rice wine vinegar
- 2 Tbsps. shallots, minced
- 1 garlic clove, minced
- ¼ tsp. white pepper, ground
- ¼ tsp. Tabasco sauce, optional
  Juice of 1 lime
  Juice of 1 orange
  Juice of 1 large grapefruit
- 4 swordfish steaks, 8 oz. each
  Lime, orange and grapefruit pieces for garnish
  Pink peppercorns for garnish

T o make the vinaigrette combine the sherry vinegar, oil, five-spice, soy sauce, rice wine vinegar, shallots, garlic, pepper and Tabasco in a mixing bowl. Add ¼ cup of the combined fruit juices, or more to taste, to the vinaigrette. Set aside.

Grill or sauté the swordfish steaks.

Garnish the fish with fruit segments and pink peppercorns.

Stir the vinaigrette and ladle over the fish just before serving.

Billi-Bi

 Sweat the onion, shallot and parsley in white wine. Add the mussels and reduce by half, add the cream and half & half. Cook until boiling, then remove from heat.

Remove the mussels and pass the liquid through a fine strainer. Heat soup on low heat and season to taste.

Before serving add the mussels and garnish with chives.

Serves 4
Preparation Time:
  25 Minutes

½ onion, chopped
¼ cup shallots, chopped
  Parsley to taste
1 cup white wine
4 lbs. mussels
1 qt. heavy cream
½ cup half & half
  Salt and pepper to
  taste
  Fresh chives, chopped,
  for garnish

THE INN AT MYSTIC

Jct. Routes 1 and 27
Mystic, Connecticut 06355
(203) 536-9604
ROOM RATES: $55–$225
AMENITIES: Sixty-eight rooms. Kitchens and suites available. Some rooms with jacuzzi, whirlpool tubs, fireplace and canopied beds. Thirteen garden-landscaped acres with a full view of Mystic Harbor. Veranda, dock, sailboats, canoes, tennis court, pool, hot spa, and extensive gardens with a walking trail.
DIRECTIONS: Take Exit 90 off I-95 onto Route 27. Go south 2 miles and turn left on Route 1. Turn left into the first driveway.

Turn-of-the-century and colonial furnishings adorn the rooms of the historic mansion built in 1904. The rooms range from the quaint and cozy to the luxurious. The romance of the inn enticed Humphrey Bogart and Lauren Bacall as guests on their honeymoon. The three main buildings all occupy their own unique corner of the lush grounds, set next to the quiet waters of Pequotsepos Cove in Mystic Harbor.

The inn is convenient to historic Mystic, with the Seaport Museum, Mystic Marine life Aquarium, shops, galleries, cruises, golf, deep-sea fishing, bike tours, wildlife sanctuaries, Revolutionary War Ft. Griswold and the Christmas Pageant.

A jewel in the crown of the inn is The Flood Tide Restaurant, a five-star experience in elegant dining. Lunch can be on the deck overlooking the harbor, complimentary tea is served at four, or start your unforgettable dinner by relaxing in the wine and piano bar.

Samples from the menu include Smoked Salmon Rosettes, Herbed Mushroom Soup, Whole Roast Pheasant for Two, and Broiled Filet Mignon with Mushroom Caps. Desserts are a specialty here, featuring Fruited Ice Cream Tulip and the flaming Strawberries Romanoff.

Lobster Madeira Crêpe

Sauté the mushrooms, shallots and parsley in butter until cooked. Add the lobster, Madeira and the heavy cream and reduce until the sauce will coat the back of a wooden spoon.

Distribute the filling evenly into each crêpe shell, reserving some sauce to top with.

Roll each crêpe and place on a warm plate. Pour remaining sauce over the tops. Garnish with fresh dill and lobster claw. Serve immediately.

Serves 6
Preparation Time:
  15 Minutes

  2 **Tbsps. butter**
  2 **tsps. shallots, finely minced**
  1 **tsp. parsley, chopped**
  6 **button mushrooms, thinly sliced**
 12 **oz. fresh lobster meat**
 ⅓ **cup Madeira wine**
 ½ **cup + 2 Tbsps. heavy cream**
  6 **crêpe shells**
  6 **small lobster claws for garnish**
    Fresh dill for garnish

TOLLGATE HILL INN

Route 202
Litchfield, Connecticut 06759
(203) 567-4545
ROOM RATES: $110–$175
AMENITIES: Fifteen rooms and 5 suites, some with working fireplaces. Full service restaurant. Two miles from Litchfield center. Continental breakfast included.
DIRECTIONS: 2 miles east of Litchfield center on Route 202.

Lose yourself in time in the romantic tavern atmosphere of this restaurant and inn set amidst dense evergreens. The 250-year-old inn was a colonial stage stop for travelers between Hartford and Albany. The rooms are decorated in true colonial fashion.

With celebrated food and a quiet, out-of-the-way setting, the Tollgate is the spot for a weekend retreat, whether coming for a meal or to stay a night or two.

The menu is quite contemporary, featuring Chicken and Sun-Dried Tomato Spring Rolls, Pumpkin Raviolis in Garlic Cream, Crispy Breast of Chicken with Granny Smith Apples, Grilled Pork Loin with Pancetta and Roasted Prime Ribeye of Beef with Fresh Horseradish.

Angel Hair Pasta with Smoked Trout, Chives and Cream

Remove the skin, bones and head from trout. Set aside. In a saucepan over low heat, reduce the cream by half. Add the chives, trout meat in pieces and salt to taste.

Cook the pasta in boiling salted water until al dente. Drain.

Toss the pasta with the trout sauce. Season with nutmeg and pepper.

Serves 4
Preparation Time:
  20 Minutes

- 1 **trout, 10 oz., smoked**
- 1½ **cups heavy cream**
- 2 **Tbsps. fresh chives, snipped**
  Salt and pepper to taste
- 1 **lb. angel hair pasta**
  Nutmeg to taste

★

Pan Roasted Lamb Loin with Minted Sun-dried Tomato Coulis

Serves 4
Preparation Time:
 30 Minutes
Cooking Time:
 20 Minutes

 2 oz. sun-dried tomatoes
 1 Tbsp. shallots, minced
 1 tsp. garlic, minced
 1 Tbsp. fresh mint,
  chopped
 1 cup lamb or beef stock
 ½ cup Chardonnay
  Salt and pepper to
  taste
 2 lbs. lamb loin,
  boneless, peeled, cut
  into 4 pieces
 1 Tbsp. peppercorns,
  crushed
 2 Tbsps. canola oil

Put the tomatoes, shallots, garlic, mint, stock, wine, salt and pepper in a saucepan and reduce to a glaze over low heat. Pour mixture into a food processor and pulse to make a chunky sauce texture. Set aside and keep warm.

Heat a sauté pan on medium high heat. Lightly coat the lamb with the peppercorns. Add the oil to the pan and sear the lamb on both sides. Place the lamb in the oven at 400° until medium-rare, about 20 minutes.

To serve, slice each piece of lamb into 6 slices and fan over a pool of sauce.

Trade Secret: Tollgate Hill chef Leon Bouteiller recommends whole wheat couscous cooked with honey and ancho chiles as an accompaniment to this dish.

Fresh Berry Cobbler

Put the berries, sugar, lemon juice and butter in a deep sauté pan. Bring to a slow boil.

In a mixing bowl, combine the remaining ingredients. Using a large spoon, drop the dough over the berry surface. Cover the entire surface with the dough pieces to give a "cobbled" effect.

Cover and cook about 12 minutes.

Serve with a dollop of fresh whipped cream.

Serves 4
Preparation Time:
15 Minutes

2 cups fresh berries
    (blueberry, raspberry
    or strawberry)
¼ cup sugar
1 Tbsp. lemon juice
4 Tbsps. butter
¼ cup yellow cornmeal
¾ cup all-purpose flour
2 tsps. baking powder
¼ tsp. salt
1 egg
⅔ cup half-and-half
    Nutmeg to taste
1 Tbsp. corn oil
    Whipped cream

★

RHODE ISLAND:
Yachts, Jazz,
and Freedom

Y ou're never more than 25 miles from saltwater when you're in Rhode Island, the country's smallest state. But the state — which measures 48 miles by 37 miles — contains about 20 percent of the country's National Historic Monuments. And here's a bit of trivia that may win you a few bets: The official name of the state is "Rhode Island and Providence Plantations."

Rhode Island was founded by people who fought the religious intolerance of the Puritans. The main founder was Roger Williams, a minister who was banished from the Massachusetts Bay Colony because of his liberal beliefs. In 1636, Williams bought some land from the Narragansett tribe and founded Providence (in gratitude for "God's Merciful Providence"). Williams stayed on good terms with the Indians, studying their language and publishing a book on the language.

By 1776, Rhode Island became the first colony to declare its independence from England.

The early settlers built ships and hunted whales. But the main source of income came from the "triangular trade." Here's how it worked: Ships brought molasses from the West Indies. In New England, the molasses was distilled into rum, then shipped to Africa, where it was used to buy slaves. The slaves were taken to the West Indies and were traded for molasses. And so the triangular cycle continued.

In time, England exerted a commercial stranglehold on the colonies by withholding its textiles. In 1790, Moses Brown figured out how to free America from dependence on England: harness the waterpower in Pawtucket to power a cotton-manufacturing plant. The problem was that the crude machinery kept breaking down.

Along came Samuel Slater to the rescue. England protected its monopoly on the manufacture of cotton cloth by refusing to allow skilled mechanics to emigrate. Slater, a crafty man, memorized all the elements of the machinery and came to America under an assumed name. He rebuilt the broken machines and adapted them. Thus was born American manufacturing. The Slater Mill is still open to visitors in Pawtucket.

Here are some highlights of a visit to Rhode Island:

PROVIDENCE — Founded in 1636 by Roger Williams, Providence is the state capital. The State House boasts the world's second largest unsupported dome (second only to St. Peter's in Rome). It also contains a Gilbert Stuart full-length portrait of George Washington and several important documents from English monarchs. The first Baptist Church is the oldest Baptist church in the nation. The Rhode Island Museum of Art contains a 10-foot statue of Buddha and 60,000 pieces of artwork. Among other attractions, Brown University contains letters written by Christopher Columbus to Spain's Queen Isabella, describing his discoveries.

PAWTUCKET — You can still see textile mills in operation — including the historic Slater Mill, which now contains a theater that features slide shows, and a classroom. The Wilkinson Mill still operates. The wealthy mill owners built homes on Quality Hill, overlooking the river and the sources of their wealth. Roger Williams Park and Zoo is the only accredited zoo in New England. The Children's Museum of New England encourages children to touch the cooking utensils in Great-Grandmother's Kitchen; it also contains a room-size map of the state.

NEWPORT — This is a center of music, yachting , major naval and Coast Guard installations, tennis and opulent mansions. In the mid-19th century, the wealthy discovered Newport and built palatial homes, including Cornelius Vanderbilt's "The Breakers," William Vanderbilt's "Marble House" and Richard Morris Hunt's "Belcourt Castle." Newport is the birthplace of the America's Cup yacht race and the Newport (now JVC) Jazz Festival. Other highlights: Touro Synagogue, the oldest surviving synagogue in the country, Trinity Church (Washington sat in pew 81), and the International Tennis Hall of Fame and Tennis Museum. Another interesting note: the pineapple is the official city symbol.

BLOCK ISLAND — A good place to get away from the hustle and bustle, Block Island was called "Isle of the Little God" by the early Indians. Features include inviting sand dunes, 365 freshwater ponds that attract 150 species of birds — and tales of pirates. Captain Kidd is said to have stashed treasure on the island.

Cyclers of the 1890's.

★

ADESSO

CALIFORNIA CUISINE
161 Cushing Street
Providence, Rhode Island
(401) 521-0770
Lunch Monday–Saturday 11:45AM–5PM
Dinner Monday–Thursday 5PM–10:30PM
      Friday–Saturday 5PM–12AM
      Sunday 4:30PM–10:30PM
AVERAGE DINNER FOR TWO: $40

T he Adesso California Cafe brings the freshness of California cuisine to the eastern seaboard. The restaurant is light and airy, with skylights, glittery steel-and-glass, floral designs and pink, gray and teal accents offset by black china. The atmosphere is stylish but unpretentious.

Specialties at the restaurant include wood-oven pizzas, dishes from the mesquite grill and fabulous pastas. Samples include Aged Sirloin Carpaccio served Rare with Black Olive Pesto, Pasta with Grilled Chicken and Italian Sausage in a Sauce of Balsamic Vinegar, Ale and Rosemary, Lobster Pizza with Champagne Sauce and Mushrooms and Grilled Salmon in Red Pepper, Vermouth and Sherry Cream Sauce.

ADESSO'S MENU FOR FOUR

Chicken Breast Salad with Artichoke and Champagne Vinaigrette

Black Pepper Linguine with Shrimp and Asparagus in Pink Vodka Sauce

Grilled Pork Chops with Honey, Ginger and Rice Wine Vinaigrette

Chicken Breast Salad with Artichoke and Champagne Vinaigrette

T rim artichokes and cut out whole bottoms. Poach the bottoms until tender in simmering water with a little lemon juice and salt. Cool and slice.

Grill the chicken and cool completely. Thinly slice the breasts.

Whisk the mustard and egg yolks together until well blended and lightened. Blend in the vinegar, garlic, rosemary and ½ cup Parmesan. Slowly add oil in a thin stream while whisking vigorously. Whisk in salt and pepper.

On individual salad plates, arrange a ring of endive, then an inner ring of radicchio. Place lettuces in the middle. Set green beans on the outer ring of the endive.

Toss the grilled chicken slices and artichoke bottoms with a small portion of the vinaigrette. Arrange on top of the lettuce.

Garnish with tomatoes, corn and remaining Parmesan. Serve with extra vinaigrette on the side.

Serves 4
Preparation Time:
  20 Minutes

  2 artichokes
    Lemon juice
    Salt for boiling water
  2 chicken breasts, whole, boneless
  2 Tbsps. Dijon mustard
  4 egg yolks
  ¾ cup champagne vinegar
  1 Tbsp. garlic, minced
  1 Tbsp. fresh rosemary, chopped
  ½ cup + 2 Tbsps. Parmesan cheese, grated
  1 cup olive oil
  ⅛ tsp. salt
  ¼ tsp. pepper
 24 spears Belgian endive
  1 small head radicchio
  6 cups assorted lettuce
  1 cup green beans, poached
  2 Tbsps. sun-dried tomatoes, julienned
  ¼ cup corn, cooked

☆

Black Pepper Linguine with Shrimp and Asparagus in Pink Vodka Sauce

Serves 4
Preparation Time:
15 Minutes

16 medium shrimp
 1 cup asparagus tips,
    lightly poached
¼ cup shallots, diced
½ cup (1 stick) butter,
    clarified
⅓ cup vodka
 2 cups plum tomatoes,
    canned, crushed
½ cup heavy cream
⅔ cup fresh basil,
    chopped
¼ cup sun-dried
    tomatoes, julienned
 1 lb. black pepper
    linguine, cooked
½ cup Parmesan cheese,
    grated

P eel and devein the shrimp, then split them lengthwise.

Sauté the shrimp, asparagus and shallots in the butter. When half cooked, deglaze with the vodka. When the alcohol has burned off, add the canned tomatoes, cream, basil and sun-dried tomatoes. Reduce by one fourth.

Add the linguine to the vodka sauce. Sprinkle with Parmesan and toss.

Grilled Pork Chops with Honey, Ginger and Rice Wine Vinaigrette

Grill the pork chops to desired doneness.
While the chops grill, combine the remaining ingredients, except the olive and sesame oils.

Slowly incorporate the oils while whisking briskly until vinaigrette is well mixed.

Spoon the vinaigrette over the cooked chops. Garnish with a sprig of thyme.

Serves 4
Preparation Time:
  30 Minutes

  8 loin pork chops, 8 oz.
    each, center cut
1½ Tbsps. honey
1½ Tbsps. fresh thyme
  1 tsp. fresh ginger,
    grated
  1 Tbsp. shallots, chopped
  2 Tbsps. soy sauce
  2 Tbsps. rice wine
    vinegar
⅓ cup chicken stock
½ tsp. garlic, minced
⅛ tsp. red pepper flakes
⅛ tsp. salt
⅛ tsp. pepper
  1 cup olive oil
¼ cup sesame oil
    Thyme for garnish

THE PLACE AT YESTERDAY'S

ECLECTIC INTERNATIONAL CUISINE
28 Washington Square
Newport, Rhode Island
(401) 847-0125
Dinner 5:30PM–10PM
AVERAGE DINNER FOR TWO: $50

ithout a doubt, The Place at Yesterday's is one of the locals' most popular restaurants — and with good reason. The Place is a wine bar and grill tucked into the corner of Yesterday's restaurant.

The theme is nostalgia, with an abundance of art deco and Tiffany hanging lamps, polished brass, dark wainscoting and authentic photos of old Newport over the booths. The food from celebrated Chef Alex Daglis, Jr. is imaginative and exciting, with a flair for presentation.

Menu highlights include Grilled Venison with a Maple Vinaigrette, Pan-Seared Red Snapper with Lobster and Guava, Southwestern Grilled Lamb Chops, Jamaican Jerk Chicken and Moroccan Halibut.

The Place at Yesterday's offers a warm, friendly atmosphere, an extensive wine list and exceptional service.

THE PLACE AT YESTERDAY'S MENU FOR FOUR

Sweet Potato Bisque with Maple Fried Chicken

Pan-Seared Halibut in a Curry Crust with Caramelized Ginger Sauce

Cranberry Bread Pudding with Warm Caramel Pecan Sauce

Spicy Sweet Potato Bisque with Maple Fried Chicken

L ightly sauté the onions and carrots for 5 minutes, add the sweet potatoes, thyme and stock. Let simmer until the sweet potatoes are very soft. Add the jalapeño. Remove from heat and let partially cool.

Place the soup in a blender in small amounts and purée while gradually adding the cream. When all the soup is puréed, add the ½ cup maple syrup, lime juice, salt and pepper. Cool until ready to serve.

Put chicken pieces in remaining maple syrup. Taking out 2 or 3 pieces at a time, roll chicken in bread crumbs, lightly patting with fingertips. These may be prepared several hours in advance.

Before serving, fry the chicken pieces in hot olive oil until golden brown. Add them to the warm soup.

Serves 4
Preparation Time:
** 30 Minutes**

- ½ cup onion, chopped
- ½ cup carrots, chopped
- 2 lbs. sweet potatoes, peeled, coarsely chopped
- ¼ tsp. thyme
- 1½ cups chicken stock
- 1 tsp. jalapeño pepper, chopped
- 2 cups heavy cream
- ½ cup + 2 Tbsps. maple syrup
- 2 Tbsps. lime juice
  Salt and pepper to taste
- ½ cup boneless chicken breast, cut into small pieces
- 1 cup bread crumbs
  Olive oil for frying

★

Halibut in a Curry Crust
with Caramelized Ginger Sauce

Serves 4
Preparation Time:
  30 Minutes

  1 **mango, peeled, finely**
     diced
  1 **papaya, seeded,**
     skinned, finely
     chopped
  ½ **small tomato, seeded,**
     finely chopped
  1 **Tbsp. red onion, finely**
     chopped
  ⅔ **cup green and red bell**
     peppers, finely
     chopped
     Olive oil for frying
  ¼ **cup brown sugar**
  2 **Tbsps. ground ginger**
  ½ **cup Marsala wine**
  1 **cup vegetable stock**
  2 **Tbsps. soy sauce**
     Salt and pepper to
     taste
  4 **Halibut steaks, 6 oz.**
     each, boneless
  3 **Tbsps. curry powder**

ake a mango-papaya salsa by combining the mango, papaya, tomato and red onion in a mixing bowl. Refrigerate immediately. Bring to room temperature before serving.

For the caramelized ginger sauce, sauté the green and red peppers in olive oil for 3 minutes. Add the brown sugar and ginger and cook 2 minutes more. Add the Marsala and reduce to ⅓ liquid. Add the stock and reduce by half. Add the soy sauce. Salt and pepper to taste. Chill until ready to serve. May be prepared one day ahead.

Season the halibut steaks with curry powder and sear in a hot pan coated with olive oil. Cook on high heat 2 minutes or until golden brown, turn and continue cooking, lowering the heat until the fish is cooked through.

To serve, place the fish in a pool of warm ginger sauce and garnish with the mango-papaya salsa.

★

Cranberry Bread Pudding
with Warm Caramel Pecan Sauce

I n a saucepan, combine 1 cup sugar, water, orange zest and vanilla. Heat to dissolve the sugar. Add the cranberries and bring the mixture to a boil. Simmer for 4 minutes. Remove from heat and cool the mixture in the refrigerator for 1 hour.

Cut the French bread into 1" chunks. Drizzle with 1 Tbsp. butter and toast until golden brown. Set aside.

In a mixing bowl, whisk together the milk, ¾ cup sugar and the eggs. Stir in the toasted bread and add the chilled cranberry mixture.

Place in an oiled casserole dish and sprinkle the top with cinnamon and ½ cup sugar. Bake at 350° for 1 hour.

In a skillet over medium-low heat, add the remaining butter and the brown sugar. Simmer for 2 minutes while stirring. Add the pecan pieces and slowly pour in the heavy cream while continuously whisking. Heat through.

Serve the pudding warm, drizzled with the warm caramel pecan sauce. May be garnished with whipped cream and sprigs of mint.

Serves 4
Preparation Time:
  30 Minutes
(note refrigeration time)
Baking Time:
  1 Hour

2¼ cups sugar
1 cup water
  Zest of one orange
1 Tbsp. vanilla extract
2 cups cranberries
1 lb. French bread
5 Tbsps. butter, melted
3 cups milk
5 eggs
2 tsps. cinnamon
½ cup brown sugar
½ cup heavy cream
¾ cup pecans, toasted, chopped
  Whipped cream, optional
  Mint sprigs for garnish

POT AU FEU

FRENCH CUISINE
44 Custom House Street
Providence, Rhode Island
(401) 273-8953
Lunch Tuesday–Friday 12PM–1:30PM
Dinner Tuesday–Friday 6PM–9PM
      Saturday 6PM–9:30PM
AVERAGE DINNER FOR TWO: $65

The Pot au Feu is somewhat of a landmark in Providence, having served the finest French food there for over twenty years. Overlooking historic Custom House Street, it now features two dining options. The downstairs Bistro is relaxing and cozy with views to the kitchen, candlelit, rich warm woods and rustic original brick walls. The upstairs Salon displays classic French elegance in pale floral shades and gilt-framed mirrors.

No details are spared in preparation and presentation from the first taste of the velvet-like foie gras to the grand wine list providing the perfect accompaniment for every course.

At the Pot au Feu, though the menu changes daily, one often can expect to find on the menu such temptations as Salad Nicoise; Grilled Boneless Lamb Loin marinated in Rosemary and Basil; Grilled Pork Tenderloin in White Wine, Calvados and Cream Sauce with Apple Slices; a quintessential Bouillabaisse; Atlantic Salmon with Raspberry Beurre Blanc; and the perfect Strawberry Soufflé.

POT AU FEU'S MENU FOR FOUR

Pâté Maison

French Onion Soup

Greens with Goat Cheese and Roasted Red Peppers

Pot au Feu

Crème Brulée

Pâté Maison

Clean and dry the livers. Sauté the onion in 1 Tbsp. butter. Add the livers, curry and paprika. Cover and cook over low heat until livers are medium-rare. Add the brandy and salt and pepper to taste.

Blend the livers and remaining butter in a food processor until smooth.

Chill until firm.

Serves 4
Preparation Time:
  10 Minutes

1½ lbs. chicken livers
  1 small onion, chopped
  1 cup (2 sticks) butter, softened
  1 Tbsp. curry powder
  2 tsps. paprika
  ¼ cup brandy
    Salt and pepper to taste

☆

French Onion Soup

Serves 4
Preparation Time:
 20 Minutes
Cooking Time:
 1 Hour, 30 Minutes

⅓ cup oil for sautéing
6 small onions
2 qts. beef stock
1 cup sherry
½ bunch fresh thyme, chopped
3 bay leaves
 Salt and pepper to taste
4 slices French bread
1 cup Gruyère cheese, grated

Heat oil in a large pot.
  Julienne the onions and add to the oil. Sauté to a golden brown. Deglaze the pot with sherry, then add the stock. Add the thyme and bay leaves and bring to a boil. Reduce to a simmer and cook for 1 to 1½ hours. Season to taste.

Ladle into individual soup crocks, top with a slice of bread and a mound of cheese. Brown cheese quickly under a broiler.

Greens with Goat Cheese and Roasted Red Peppers

Spread goat cheese onto baguette slices and place in a warm oven until cheese melts.

Place on top of mixed greens and herbs with pepper slices on the side. Dress with balsamic vinegar and olive oil.

Serves 4
Preparation Time:
15 Minutes

- 8 oz. goat cheese
- 4 slices baguette
- 2 red bell peppers, roasted, sliced
- 1 lb. salad greens
  Herbs of choice
  Balsamic vinegar
  Olive oil

Pot au Feu

Serves 4
Preparation Time:
 30 Minutes
Cooking Time:
 2 Hours 30 Minutes

1½ lbs. beef, cut into 2"
   chunks
 1 cup beef stock
¼ cup tomato paste
 1 chicken, 2 lbs., cut into
   8 pieces
 1 qt. chicken stock
¾ lb. carrots, peeled, cut
   into large pieces
 2 lbs. onions, quartered
½ bunch celery, cut into
   large pieces
½ cabbage head, cored,
   cut into 8 pieces
 1 leek, cut into 1" or 2"
   pieces
 1 sachet bag containing
   bay leaf, thyme,
   parsley stems, cloves,
   black peppercorns,
   nutmeg, mace
 8 medium potatoes, cut
   into large pieces
 1 lb. beef marrow bones,
   optional
   Dijon mustard for side
   Grated horseradish for
   side

Braise the beef with beef stock and tomato paste. Simmer for 2 hours or until the beef is tender.

In a separate pot, simmer together the chicken, chicken stock, carrots, onions, celery, cabbage, leek and seasonings for 1 to 1½ hours. In the last half hour, add the potatoes.

Combine the beef and chicken mixtures. Add the bones if desired and simmer for 30 minutes.

Skim the broth and strain into individual serving bowls. Arrange chicken, beef and vegetables on a large platter.

Serve with small bowls of Dijon mustard and grated horseradish.

☆

Crème Brulée

Heat the cream with the vanilla bean to a boil. Whisk the egg yolks and ½ cup sugar until light. Add the cream to the egg yolks.

Pour into 4 shallow bowls. Bake in a water bath at 300° until firm, about 40 minutes. Refrigerate for at least 2 hours.

When ready to serve, sprinkle 1 Tbsp. sugar on the top of each bowl and place under a broiler until top is browned.

Serves 4
Preparation Time:
20 Minutes
(note refrigeration time)
Cooking Time:
45 Minutes

4 cups heavy cream
1 vanilla bean, split
¾ cup sugar
8 egg yolks

THE WHITE HORSE TAVERN

CONTINENTAL/AMERICAN ELEGANT CUISINE
Marlborough & Farewell Streets
Newport, Rhode Island
(401) 849-3600
Lunch Wednesday–Monday 12PM–3PM
Dinner 6PM–10PM
AVERAGE DINNER FOR TWO: $100

Step back in time at the exclusive White Horse Tavern. Built in 1637, it is America's oldest tavern and now offers some of the most elegant dining in all of New England. The Rhode Island general assembly and criminal court met in the tavern in the mid-eighteenth century. Its clapboard walls, gambrel roof, giant inner beams and cavernous fireplaces exemplify seventeenth century American design. The White Horse Tavern offers an exquisite menu which features both the best of New England and tastes of the continent.

A tradition at the White Horse Tavern is the Champagne Sunday Brunch which, in addition to the fresh fruit and freshly baked breads and muffins, includes New England Chicken, Clam Stew and Old English Mixed Grill. Dinner highlights include Tavern Gravlax, Grilled Atlantic Salmon, Veal Tenderloin in a Potato Nest and Roasted Poussin.

THE WHITE HORSE TAVERN'S MENU FOR FOUR

Grilled Summer Bisque

Grilled Veal Tenderloin in Potato Nest

Triple Silk

Grilled Summer Bisque

Grill the corn, fennel and tomatoes. Remove kernels from grilled corn cobs. Set aside.

In a stock pot over medium heat, sauté the onions until transparent. Add the grilled tomatoes, fennel and half the corn kernels. Cook for 10 minutes, stirring constantly. Remove from heat and puree the mixture.

Return the pureed vegetables to the stock pot. Add the chicken stock and sour cream. Heat until soup is hot. Season to taste with salt and pepper.

Garnish with remaining corn kernels and chopped fennel.

Serves 4
Preparation time:
  45 Minutes

  8 ears of corn, husked
  3 fennel bulbs
  8 tomatoes, quartered
  2 onions, chopped
  3 cups chicken stock
  2 cups sour cream
    Salt and pepper
  $\frac{1}{2}$ cup fennel tops,
    chopped

Grilled Veal Tenderloin in Potato Nest

Serves 4
Preparation Time:
  1 Hour 15 Minutes

  5 potatoes, peeled,
     julienne
  4 cups canola oil
  2 cups veal demi-glace
  1 egg
  1 tsp. Dijon mustard
1⅓ cups olive oil
  4 Tbsps. lemon juice
  ⅓ cup fresh sage,
     chopped
  4 veal tenderloins, 8 oz.
     each
  3 bunches of arugula
     Balsamic vinegar
     Salt and white pepper
     Zest of 2 lemons

L ightly salt julienne potatoes and drain off excess liquid. Heat the canola oil in a sauce pan over medium heat and fry the potatoes until golden brown. Remove from heat and drain the potatoes on a paper towel.

In a saucepan, reduce the demi-glace until it coats the back of a spoon, set aside.

In a food processor or mixing bowl, combine the egg and Dijon mustard together. Slowly drizzle in 1 cup of olive oil until mixture is the consistency of mayonnaise. Add the lemon juice and sage to taste.

Trim veal tenderloins and cut into 2" medallions. Pound to slightly increase size and grill quickly over high flame to sear.

Whisk together the reduced demi-glace and vinaigrette mixture and pool onto plates. Toss arugula with balsamic vinegar and remaining ⅓ cup olive oil, season lightly with salt and white pepper. Arrange on the plate and top with potato sticks to create a nest. Place grilled veal medallions in nest and garnish with lemon zest.

Triple Silk

 n a mixing bowl, beat egg yolks and 1 cup sugar until mixture forms ribbons from lifted spoon. Set aside.

Dissolve gelatin in ⅔ cup water. Set aside.

Add the remaining ⅓ cup sugar into the light cream and scald the mixture over medium heat.

Stir the gelatin into the yolks and add the scalded light cream.

Place each of the three chocolates into three separate bowls. Divide the cream mixture evenly among the three bowls. Melt each over a double boiler, stirring constantly. When chocolates are melted, fold the whipped cream evenly among the three bowls.

Pour one chocolate mixture into a 10" springform pan and freeze. Repeat with each successive layer.

Trade Secret: This elegant dessert is even more special if served with a puree of fresh fruit or melba sauce spiked with brandy.

Serves 4
Preparation Time:
  3 Hours

  7 egg yolks
1⅓ cups sugar
  2 Tbsps. gelatin
1⅓ cups light cream
  8 oz. white chocolate
  8 oz. milk chocolate
  8 oz. dark chocolate
  1 qt. heavy cream,
     whipped
 ⅔ cup water

THE MELVILLE HOUSE

39 Clarke Street
Newport, Rhode Island 02840
(401) 847-0640
ROOM RATES: $45–$110
AMENITIES: Seven rooms. Complimentary breakfast and tea time snack. Bicycles available for guests.
DIRECTIONS: Once in Newport, follow the signs to the Gateway Visitors Center. At the Visitors Center intersection, turn left onto W. Marlborough Street. Turn right at the first stop sign, Thames Street. Turn left at the first light, Touro Street. Turn right onto Clarke Street (one-way). The Melville House is at the end, on the right.

Built around 1750, The Melville House is located in the heart of the Historic Hill section of Newport, the streets of which are still lit with gas lamps. The French General Rochambeau quartered some of his troops here when they fought in the Revolutionary War under George Washington.

The Melville House sits on one of the quietest streets in Newport, and yet is only a block from Thames Street and the harborfront where many of the city's finest restaurants, antique shops and galleries can be found. It is also within walking distance to Newport's many historic places of worship, such as Touro Synagogue (the oldest in the country), Trinity Church (built in 1726) and St. Mary's Church (where President John F. Kennedy married Jacqueline). The Tennis Hall of Fame, the famous and lavish mansions of the Vanderbilts, Astors and the Belmonts, the Naval War College and Newport's finest ocean beaches are just minutes away.

The rooms of The Melville House are furnished in traditional Colonial style, offering guests a classic New England stay.

Pumpkin Chocolate Chip Muffins

Thoroughly mix dry ingredients in a large bowl. Set aside.

In a smaller bowl, mix together the eggs, pumpkin and butter, blending well. Stir in the chocolate chips.

Pour the pumpkin mixture into the dry ingredients and fold with a spatula until just moist.

Spoon into muffin tin or cups and bake at 350° for 25 minutes.

Serves 6
Preparation Time:
  15 Minutes
Baking Time:
  25 Minutes

3⅓ cups all-purpose flour
1½ cups sugar
  2 Tbsps. pumpkin pie
     spice
  2 tsps. baking soda
  1 tsp. baking powder
½ tsp. salt
  4 eggs, large, lightly
     beaten
  2 cups pumpkin, canned
  1 cup butter, melted
1½ cups chocolate chips

Irish Raisin Scones

Serves 4
Preparation Time:
  25 Minutes
Baking Time:
  20 Minutes

  4 cups all-purpose flour
¾ cup sugar
  4 tsps. baking powder,
¼ tsp. baking soda
  1 tsp. salt
¼ cup (½ stick) butter,
    sliced
1½ cups raisins
  1 egg
  2 Tbsps. sour cream
  2 cups buttermilk
    Sugar to taste

ix dry ingredients together. Work the sliced butter into the flour mixture until well blended. Add raisins and mix well by hand. Set aside.

In a small bowl, beat together the egg, sour cream and buttermilk.

Pour the milk mixture slowly into the flour mixture while constantly stirring with a fork.

Roll the dough out onto a floured surface, knead for 2 minutes and form into a ball. Divide the dough in half and form each half into a flat disk. Cut each disk with a pastry cutter into 6 triangles and place on an ungreased baking sheet.

Bake at 425° for about 20 minutes or until golden brown and firm.

Brush with melted butter and sprinkle with sugar.

Sourdough Bread

Soften yeast in the warm water for five minutes.
In a large bowl, combine the starter, yeast and water, dry milk, butter, sugar, salt and 3 cups flour. Beat the mixture until smooth, then cover with a cloth and let stand for approx. 1 hour, until bubbly and doubled in size.

Stir in the remaining flour, or enough to make a workable dough. Turn out on a floured board and knead for ten minutes until smooth, adding flour, if needed.

Cut into two pieces and let rest while greasing 2 large bread pans.

Form into loaves, place in pans and brush the tops with oil. Cover with a cloth and let rise approximately 1½ hours until double.

Bake at 375° for 50 minutes until golden brown. Remove from pan and place on racks to cool.

Trade Secret: For an interesting sour flavor, add three tablespoons of buttermilk, plain yogurt or sour cream. Vary the texture by substituting the flour with rye and/or stone ground wheat.

Serves 4
Preparation Time:
   20 Minutes
(note rising time)
Baking Time:
   50 Minutes

   1 Tbsp. active dry yeast
3½ cups sourdough starter
   ½ cup warm water
   3 Tbsps. non-fat dry
      milk
   4 Tbsps. butter, melted
   4 Tbsps. sugar
   3 tsps. salt
   6 cups flour
      Oil

☆

SHELTER HARBOR INN

Route 1, 10 Wagner Road
Westerly, Rhode Island 02891
(401) 322-8883
ROOM RATES: $88–$112
AMENITIES: Twenty-three rooms, seven with fireplaces, hot tub with water view, meeting facilities, 2 paddle tennis courts, croquet court, bocci, access to private beach, full restaurant, near tennis, boating, amusements, shopping.
DIRECTIONS: Between Mystic and Newport. Follow Route 78 to the traffic lights. Turn left onto Rt. 1 North, and go 4 miles to the entrance of Shelter Harbor on the right.

T he Shelter Harbor Inn sits on one of the most beautiful stretches of Rhode Island shoreline. Originally an 1800s farm, fields and stone walls surround the inn in peaceful tranquillity. The farm became a music center in 1911 and is now a comfortable, unpretentious country inn emphasizing relaxation, good food and a warm, friendly atmosphere. The main house has ten guest rooms with private baths, some with fireplaces and private decks. The barn has been converted into ten rooms, also with private baths, and the carriage house also hosts rooms, each with its own fireplace.

All guests have access to a third floor deck with a hot tub and panoramic views of Block Island Sound. The main house has been beautifully restored and includes the living room, reception area and library, as well as a sun porch and dining room overlooking the rear gardens. Elegant country dining is the pride of the inn, with a complete selection of wines to complement Chef Joe Collins' traditional New England fare. Breakfast, lunch and dinner are served daily.

Hazelnut Chicken with Orange Thyme Cream

Remove peel and white pith from the oranges. Cut between membranes with a small, sharp knife, releasing orange segments.

Using a flat mallet or rolling pin, pound the chicken between 2 sheets of waxed paper to ½" thick.

Combine the hazelnuts, bread crumbs and ½ tsp. thyme on a large plate. Dip the chicken pieces in flour, shaking off the excess. Dip into egg, then hazelnut mixture, shaking off excess.

Melt the butter in a heavy skillet over medium heat. Add the chicken and cook until golden brown and springy to the touch, about 3 minutes per side. Transfer to plates and cover with foil to keep warm.

Stir the cream, orange juice, liqueur and ¼ tsp. thyme into skillet and bring to a boil. Reduce heat and simmer until reduced by half. Season to taste.

Spoon sauce over chicken, garnish with orange segments and serve.

Serves 4
Preparation Time:
  30 Minutes

- 2 large oranges
- 2 whole chicken breasts, boned, skinned, halved
- ⅔ cup hazelnuts, husked, finely chopped
- ⅔ cup bread crumbs
- ¾ tsp. dried thyme
  All-purpose flour for coating
- 2 eggs, beaten with 2 Tbsps. water
- 6 Tbsps. (¾ stick) butter, unsalted
- 2 cups heavy cream
- 1 cup orange juice
- 2 Tbsps. Frangelico liqueur
  Salt and pepper to taste

☆

MASSACHUSETTS: Enormous Impact on America

Massachusetts is so steeped in history that it's impossible to discuss the formation of America without discussing the state. The Pilgrims, who had set sail for Virginia, drifted off course and landed at Cape Cod instead. Finding the land inhospitable, they set sail again and landed at Plymouth on Dec. 21, 1620. The first person to step ashore is reputed to be a young girl, Mary Chilton.

We won't recount the complex history of the area — we'll leave that to the history books. But consider these Massachusetts names and you'll see what an enormous influence they had on the country: Paul Revere, John Hancock, Samuel Adams, Cotton Mather, Benjamin Franklin, Ralph Waldo Emerson, Henry David Thoreau, Nathaniel Hawhtorne, Oliver Wendell Homes and John F. Kennedy. Why the enormous impact? Perhaps the best explanation is that Massachusetts contains over 100 institutions of higher learning.

And consider these historic Massachusetts sites: Boston, Bunker Hill, New Bedford, Cape Cod, Nantucket, Martha's Vineyard, Harvard, Walden Pond, Woods Hole, Hyannis Port, Salem, the Massachusetts Institute of Technology, Lexington, Concord and Lake Chargoggagoggmanchauggagogg-gchaubunagungamaugg, the longest geographic name in America.

The state is so rich in history that we can only mention the highlights.

BOSTON — Originally called Trimountain for three nearby hills, Boston is the core of the state. Immigrants from all over the world came to Boston, then later spread throughout the country. Boston, long a leader in the arts and sciences, boasts some of the finest museums: the Museum of Fine Arts, noted for its Impressionist paintings; the Isabella Stewart Gardner Museum, a reconstructed 15th-century Venetian palace loaded with fine art; the Computer Museum, which houses old and new machines; and the John Fitzgerald Kennedy Library, which houses a model of the PT-109, films and memorabilia of JFK's career.

Architectural highlights include the 19th-century brownstone town houses of Beacon Hill; Charles Bullfinch's gold-domed State House, built in 1798; Faneuil Hall (the locals pronounce it Fan'l), given to the city in 1742, which contains a food market downstairs and a meeting hall on the top floor; the Old North Church (1723), the oldest church in

Feeding the swans in Boston's Public Garden, with a swan boat in the background, circa 1920.

McGreevy's 3rd Base Saloon.

Photos from the Boston Public Library.

Boston; the impressive John Hancock Tower, designed by I.M. Pei; and the Christian Science Church, established in 1894 by Mary Baker Eddy.

Perhaps the best way to see many of the historic sites is to walk the 2½-mile long Freedom Trail. Marked by a red line painted on the sidewalk, the trail passes 22 of Boston's most significant buildings, monuments and historic sites, including Boston Common, the oldest park in America; the Park Street Church, built in 1809 and later the site of an early speech protesting slavery; the Old Granary Burial Ground, where Paul Revere and many other historic figures are buried; the Benjamin Franklin Statue; the Old State House, where the Declaration of Independence was first read to the citizens; the site of the Boston Massacre; Faneuil Hall, called the "cradle of Liberty;" the Paul Revere House; Paul Revere Mall; the Old North Church, reputed to be the church where lanterns announced the arrival of the British; and the USS Constitution, the historic frigate known as Old Ironsides.

Other Boston highlights worth seeing include the Swan Boat rides on the lake in the Public Garden; the Boston Aquarium, which includes a 180,000 gallon tank; the Boston Tea Party Ship and Museum; and the Children's Museum, with hands-on exhibits that help explain computers, video cameras and other wonders.

CAMBRIDGE — Home of Harvard University (1636) the oldest college in America; and the Massachusetts Institute of Technology, designed by and for scientists. While at Harvard, visit the Fogg Museum, which contains over 80,000 works of art; and the Busch-Reisinger Museum, which features a sculpture garden and European art treasures. The Widener Library contains 10 million volumes and treasures such as Shakespeare folios and a Gutenberg Bible. MIT features two of Eero Saarinen's designs, the Kresge Auditorium and the MIT Chapel.

LEXINGTON — Established in 1642, Lexington boasts many preserved colonial buildings. The Minutemen confronted the British in the village green in 1775. Check out the Museum of Our National Heritage.

CONCORD — Site of the first real battle of the American Revolution. A film at the Minuteman National Historical Park helps put the events in perspective. About a mile out of town

The Union Oyster House in Boston, established in 1826.

is Walden Pond, where Thoreau lived, wrote and contemplated. Alas, it's no longer so bucolic, but still worth a trip.

SALEM — One of the most beautiful and best preserved of the old towns, Salem was the site of the infamous witchcraft trials, during which 200 people were found guilty. Displays at the Witch Museum explain it all. Also look for the Witch House, home of the judge at the trials.

CAPE COD — A very popular tourist destination, Cape Cod (shaped like a flexed arm), contains Falmouth, a Quaker center; Woods Hole, one of the world's preeminent oceanographic research centers; Hyannis, home of the Kennedy family's summer compound; the beautiful Cape Cod National Seashore; and the artist's colony of Provincetown.

MARTHA'S VINEYARD — Vineyard Haven is the island's principal port. Edgartown is the oldest community, founded in 1642. A ferryboat, named On Time, despite the fact that it has no fixed schedule, takes passengers from Edgartown to Chappaquiddick Island.

NANTUCKET — At one time the greatest whaling port in the world, the quiet island features cobbled streets and fine old sea captains' homes.

Room D at Crosby's in Boston.

A convivial dinner party, circa 1890.

A shipment of watermelons going to market.

DALI

SPANISH CUISINE
415 Washington Street
Somerville, Massachusetts
(617) 661-3254
Dinner Sunday–Thursday 5:30PM–10PM
        Friday–Saturday 5:30PM–10:30PM
AVERAGE DINNER FOR TWO: $40

O ld-world Spanish charm, a medieval mood and the spirit of Salvador Dali engulf the rooms in atmosphere at Dali. An abundance of polished cooking utensils, as well as dried herbs hang from the walls and ceiling of the bar, interspersed with the color of giant sunflowers and lilies. Traditional masks and ceremonial decorations from regions throughout Spain add to the charm. Chef/owner Mario Leon-Iriarte and his wife and co-owner Tamara Bourso have put endless creative touches on both the decor and the food.

The specialty of the house is Tapas, small dishes like appetizers, but often combined in an order to make a meal. The list of Tapas is extensive and includes Asparagus Flan, Pork Sausages in Piquant Fig Chutney, Portuguese Corn Bread, Octopus Tentacles with Lemon and Paprika, Marinated Olives with Caper Berries, Baked Goat Cheese and New Zealand Green-Lipped Mussels with Avocado Sauce.

The entrée menu at Dali features Baked Sea Bass, Braised Rabbit in Sweet and Sour Sauce, a mix of Shrimp, Chicken and Lobster in Saffron-Tomato-Wine Sauce and Roast Lamb Marinated in Spiced Sherry and Lemon Juice.

DALI'S MENU FOR SIX

Cold Almond and Cucumber Soup

Garden Paella

Caramelized Baby Eggplant

Cold Almond & Cucumber Soup

I n a blender or food processor, blend almonds, garlic and salt with a little vegetable stock until almonds turn milky. Add the cucumber, then slowly the oil and then the vinegar. Finally, add the rest of the vegetable stock.

Serve very cold and garnish with grapes.

Trade Secret: This delicious and easy to prepare cold soup is from Andalucia, in the south of Spain.

Serves 6
Preparation Time:
  20 Minutes

¾ cup blanched almonds
3 garlic cloves, peeled
1 tsp. salt
4 cups vegetable stock
½ cucumber, peeled, seeded
5 Tbsps. olive oil
4 Tbsps. sherry or wine vinegar
18 red or green seedless grapes

Garden Paella

Serves 4
Preparation Time:
  45 Minutes
Cooking Time:
  30 Minutes

¼ cup olive oil
1 large onion, chopped
1 red pepper, chopped
3 garlic cloves, crushed
½ tsp. thyme
¼ tsp. oregano
2 bay leaves, whole
  Salt and pepper to
  taste
1½ cups short grain rice
3½ cups vegetable stock
  Pinch of saffron
  strands
1 zucchini, cut into
  ¼" slices
1 summer squash, cut
  into ¼" slices
6 broccoli florets
4 cherry tomatoes
2 artichoke hearts,
  quartered
¼ cup small green peas
  for garnish

n a large pan, heat olive oil and sauté onion, red pepper and garlic. Add thyme, oregano, bay leaves, salt and pepper.

In a paella pan or similar pan, heat 1 Tbsp. oil. Brown rice until coated and opaque. Add mixture from the first pan. Mix well.

Add saffron to vegetable stock. Place in paella pan and bring to a boil. Lower heat. Arrange zucchini, summer squash, broccoli, tomatoes and artichoke hearts on top of rice. Cover and simmer for 20 minutes.

Uncover, add peas, and simmer for 5 more minutes. Let settle for a few minutes before serving.

Trade Secret: To best extract the flavor from saffron, wrap it in foil and keep it in a warm place to dry. Then mix with warm stock.

Caramelized Baby Eggplant

T hinly slice eggplant lengthwise, leaving them attached at the tops, to be fanned out later.

Bring water to a boil. Add sugar, rum, vanilla, cinnamon and lemon. Boil until water becomes lightly syrupy.

Add eggplants and cook gently for about 10 minutes, until done but slightly firm.

Remove eggplants and continue boiling syrup until it becomes heavy. Remove from heat.

Return eggplants to syrup and cool in refrigerator.

Serve fanned out on a shallow plate with a dollop of sour cream or yogurt and a sprig of fresh mint.

Trade Secret: This sweet dish is a Basque dish with Moorish influence from Northern Spain.

Serves 6
Preparation Time:
  35 Minutes
(note refrigeration time)
Cooking Time:
  10 Minutes

  2 lbs. Japanese
    eggplants, small
  1 qt. water
 ½ cup sugar
  1 Tbsp. rum
  1 Tbsp. vanilla extract
  1 cinnamon stick
    Small pieces of lemon
    rind
 ¾ cup sour cream or
    yogurt
    Sprigs of fresh mint for
    garnish

EAST COAST GRILL

EQUATORIAL CUISINE AND SOUTHERN BARBECUE
1271 Cambridge Street
Cambridge, Massachusetts
(617) 491-6568
Dinner Sunday–Thursday 5:30PM–10PM
       Friday–Saturday 5:30PM–10:30PM
AVERAGE DINNER FOR TWO: $40

Hot, hotter and "from hell" are the menu designators at one of the world's top barbecue eateries. The storefront restaurant is brightly lit and the air is filled with the smell of southern spices and the sound of cowboy music. The tables are prepared for the fare, covered in linoleum and garnished with a bottle of the house hot sauce, "Inner Beauty." The waiters set the tone in T-shirts saying, "Grills Just Want to Have Fun."

Owners Chris Schlesinger and Cary Wheaton set a new trend for Boston when they opened the grill. They frequently host special nights like Island Night, Eat With Your Hands, and an April Fool's Gala with china and tuxedos. Schlesinger, also the chef at the grill, is co-author of the book, *The Thrill of the Grill*.

Besides traditional BBQ plates and "Damn Good Fries," specialties include Two Large Moons of Pain with Dragon's Breath Dipping Sauce, The Antidote (for a $2 wimp surcharge), Poulet Yassa of Senegal with Pili Pili Sauce, Sik Sik Wat Skirt Steak, Cold-Hot Carrot Salad, Cool Cucumber Purée and Fiery Cinnamon Baked Apples with Toasted Pecans and Whipped Cream.

EAST COAST GRILL'S MENU FOR FOUR

Tangerine Glazed Grilled Shrimp Skewer

Java Salad

Dried Fruit & Apple Salad

Stuffed Quail with Brussels Sprouts, New Potatoes

Pumpkin Bread Pudding

Tangerine Glazed Grilled Shrimp Skewer

Combine tangerine juice, ginger, garlic and lime juice in a sauce pan and reduce by ⅔. Strain and cool.

Peel and devein the shrimp. Thread 4 per skewer. Lightly brush with oil and season to taste. Grill over medium heat, 3 to 4 minutes per side.

When done, generously coat with tangerine glaze and sprinkle with peanuts.

Serves 4
Preparation Time:
  15 Minutes

  4 cups tangerine juice
  1 tsp. fresh ginger, minced
  1 tsp. fresh garlic, minced
    Juice of 1 lime
 16 medium shrimp
    Oil for grilling
  ¼ cup peanuts, ground

Java Slaw

Serves 4
Preparation Time:
15 Minutes

2 cups green cabbage, shredded

1 cup carrots, peeled, shredded

½ cup bean sprouts

½ cup peanuts, toasted, ground

1 Tbsp. fresh ginger, minced

1 Tbsp. hot chile pepper, minced

1 tsp. garlic, minced

2 Tbsps. coriander seeds, toasted, ground

¼ cup sugar

¼ cup soy sauce

¼ cup molasses

¼ cup peanut oil

Salt and pepper to taste

P ut cabbage, carrots, sprouts and peanuts in a large mixing bowl.

Put remaining ingredients in a food processor and blend well. Pour over vegetables and mix well.

☆

Dried Fruit and Apple Salad

Put raisins in wine and water for at least 15 minutes to soak.

Chop ginger extremely fine and mix in a large bowl with the apple wedges, almonds, brown sugar and spices. Add raisins, lime juice, cilantro, salt and pepper.

If the salad appears dry, add 1 Tbsp. at a time of the water and wine mixture until desired consistency. Reseason if necessary.

Serves 4
Preparation Time:
 20 Minutes

- 2 cups raisins and/or dried fruit
- ½ cup red wine
- ½ cup warm water
- 1 tsp. ginger, chopped
- 6 apples, cut into wedges
- ½ cup almonds, toasted
- ¼ cup brown sugar
- ½ tsp. coriander, toasted, ground
- ½ tsp. cumin, toasted, ground
- ½ tsp. cayenne
  Juice of 2 limes
- ¼ cup cilantro, chopped
  Salt and pepper to taste

Stuffed Quail with Brussels Sprouts and New Potatoes

Serves 4
Preparation Time:
  45 Minutes

  2 hot Italian sausages,
     4 oz. each
 ½ cup celery, finely diced
  2 Tbsps. + 2 tsps. garlic,
     minced
 ½ cup white onion, finely
     diced
 ¾ cup olive oil
  8 quail, boned
  2 Tbsps. shallots,
     chopped
 12 medium new potatoes
 40 Brussels sprouts
 ½ cup balsamic vinegar
 ½ cup chicken stock
  2 cups red cabbage,
     shredded
     Salt and pepper to
     taste

R emove casing from sausages and crumble the meat into small pieces.
  Heat the olive oil in a sauté pan over medium-high heat. Add 2 tsps. garlic, cook for about 30 seconds, add celery and sauté for 1 minute more. Add the sausage and continue to sauté until the sausage is fully cooked, about 3 minutes. Cool. Stuff the quails with the sausage mixture.

Blanch the new potatoes and Brussels sprouts, separately, until easily pierced with a fork.

Heat the remaining oil in a sauté pan over medium-high heat. When oil is hot, add the quail and fry for about 3 minutes until golden brown. Flip the quail and add the remaining garlic, shallots, potatoes and Brussels spouts. Sauté about 3 minutes more, shaking the pan to prevent burning.

When done, remove the ingredients and place on serving plates. Return pan to heat and deglaze with vinegar. Add the chicken stock and red cabbage. Simmer 2 minutes, season with salt and pepper.

Pour over the quail and vegetables.

Pumpkin Bread Pudding with Maple Brown Sugar Caramel Sauce

Prepare the custard by combining the eggs, milk, cream, vanilla, cinnamon, nutmeg, allspice, sugar to taste and pumpkin purée in a mixing bowl.

Put the cornbread and raisins in a baking pan. Pour the custard over the bread. Let stand 15 minutes.

Cover with aluminum foil and place in a large roasting pan with water 2/3 up the sides of the baking pan.

Bake at 350° for 1 to 1½ hours, rotating every half hour until it starts to firm. Remove the foil and continue to bake until firm to the touch. Remove from heat and cool.

In a sauce pan, combine the brown sugar, butter, syrup and water. Bring mixture to a boil to the consistency of a thick maple syrup.

Serve the pudding cold with warm sauce.

Trade Secret: This dish works best made 1 to 2 days ahead of time, with the sauce heated in a water bath or microwave.

Serves 4
Preparation Time:
  20 Minutes
Cooking Time:
  1 Hour, 30 Minutes

  6 eggs, beaten
  2 cups milk
  ¼ cup heavy cream
  2 tsps. vanilla extract
  1 Tbsp. cinnamon
  1 tsp. nutmeg
  ½ tsp. allspice
  1 to 2 cups sugar
  3 cups pumpkin purée, canned or fresh
  4 cups cornbread, stale, large crumbles
  2 cups raisins
  2 cups brown sugar, packed
  1 cup (2 sticks) butter, unsalted
  ½ cup maple syrup
  1½ cups water

★

HAMMERSLEY'S BISTRO

BISTRO CUISINE
553 Tremont Street
Boston, Massachusetts
(617) 423-2700
Dinner Sunday–Thursday 6PM–10PM
      Friday–Saturday 6PM–10:30PM
AVERAGE DINNER FOR TWO: $90

H ammersley's Bistro has become a Boston South End landmark. The simple but tasteful atmosphere features basic black, white and fire-engine-red lacquer with white paper tablecloths and oversize French and Spanish art posters. The aromas and energy flow into the dining room from the open kitchen, where all the staff sport the trademark red base-ball caps. Although the restaurant sits in a comfortable neighborhood, it is just around the corner from the boutiques and shops of the Back Bay and the Copley Place department stores.

Chef/owner Gordon Hammersley has grown famous by exercising his unique talent in tak-ing traditional earthy bistro dishes and adding a touch of sophistication for today's taste. Examples of Hammersley's award-winning bistro dining include the Mushroom and Garlic Sandwich, Onion Soup Puréed with Carrots, Garlic and Red Wine, Penne Pasta with Vegetables in Garlic Cream Sauce, Veal Chops Marinated in Mustard and Onions in a Sherry Reduction, Pork Tenderloin Roasted with Prunes and Pears in Madeira Sauce, Stuffed Leg of Lamb with Olive, Kale and Pepper and French Chocolate Cake with Hazelnut Ice Cream. The world-class wine list complements the quality of the food.

HAMMERSLEY'S BISTRO'S MENU FOR SIX

Veal Stew with Tarragon, Carrots and Peas

Tuna with Garlic, Olive and Sun-Dried Tomato Compote

Brown Butter and Almond Tart

Veal Stew with Tarragon, Carrots and Peas

In a 4½ qt. casserole, brown the meat in batches in the oil over medium-high heat, seasoning with salt and pepper. Remove the meat from the casserole and put in the onion, garlic, carrots, celery, herbs, tarragon, and tomato paste. Sauté for 3 to 4 minutes, stirring occasionally. Add the meat, wine and chicken stock to the pot and just cover with water. Bring the stew to a simmer, then place in the oven at 325° for 2 hours, until the meat is tender.

Season to taste. Add the peas and top with fresh chopped tarragon.

Trade Secret: The quality of the stew meat can make quite a difference in the success of this stew.

Serves 6
Preparation Time:
  30 Minutes
Cooking Time:
  2 Hours

3 lbs. veal stew meat,
  2" cubed
  Vegetable oil for
  browning
  Kosher salt and pepper
  to taste
1 onion, chopped
2 garlic cloves, chopped
3 carrots, peeled,
  1" sliced
1 celery stalk, peeled,
  1" sliced
1 tsp. Herbs de Provence
1 tsp. dried tarragon
1 tsp. tomato paste
1 cup white wine
2 cups chicken stock
  Water to cover
1 cup green peas, sugar
  peas or fava beans,
  cooked
  Fresh tarragon,
  chopped

Tuna with Garlic, Olive and Sun-Dried Tomato Compote

Serves 6
Preparation Time:
  20 Minutes
Cooking Time:
  20 Minutes

- ½ cup garlic cloves, whole, peeled
- 1 cup olive oil
- ½ cup black olives, pitted
- ½ cup sun-dried tomatoes, thickly sliced, soaked, drained
- 1 Tbsp. shallots, chopped
- ¼ cup balsamic vinegar
- 2 Tbsps. fresh mint, chopped
  Kosher salt and pepper to taste
- 6 tuna steaks, 6 oz. each, 1" thick

In a heavy saucepan, bring the garlic and olive oil slowly to a simmer and cook the garlic until tender and golden, about 15 minutes. Drain. Reserve oil. Combine the garlic with the olives, tomatoes, shallots, vinegar, mint, salt and pepper. Use the garlic oil to taste in making the compote. It may be served warm or at room temperature.

Salt and pepper the tuna before searing in a hot sauté pan or grilling. Cook 2 to 3 minutes each side.

Before serving, spoon the compote over the tuna steaks.

Trade Secret: Save the remaining garlic oil for use in other dishes. Roasted potatoes or a simple pasta make a great accompaniment to this dish.

Brown Butter and Almond Tart

Grind the almonds with 1 Tbsp. sugar. Set aside.
Whisk together the egg, ⅓ cup sugar and flour. Set aside.

Heat the butter until dark brown and then add the vanilla. Whisk the butter and vanilla into the egg mixture. Let cool slightly, then stir in the pastry cream, almond extract and ground almonds, reserving a little for topping.

Spread the mixture in the shell and top with almonds. Bake at 350° for about 50 minutes or until the crust is lightly browned. Let cool before serving.

Pastry Cream
Combine the milk, sugar, cornstarch, egg yolks, and the seeds from the vanilla bean in a medium-size saucepan. Place it over low heat and cook, stirring, until the mixture is simmering and thick, 3 to 5 minutes. Cook another minute and remove from the heat. Stir in the butter and salt.

Serves 6
Preparation Time:
  10 Minutes
Cooking Time:
  50 Minutes

  6 Tbsps. almonds
  ⅓ cup + 1 Tbsp. sugar
  1 egg
  ¼ cup flour
  4 Tbsps. (½ stick) butter
  1 tsp. vanilla extract
  ⅓ cup pastry cream,
    recipe follows
  2 tsps. almond extract
    Tart shell, pre-cooked

Pastry Cream:
  1 cup milk
  ½ cup granulated sugar
  2 Tbsps. cornstarch
  2 egg yolks
  ½ vanilla bean
  1 Tbsp. unsalted butter
  ⅛ tsp. salt

★

THE HARVEST

NEW AMERICAN CUISINE
44 Brattle Street
Cambridge, Massachusetts
(617) 492-1115
Dinner Sunday–Thursday 5:30PM–10PM
        Friday–Saturday 5:30PM–11PM
AVERAGE DINNER FOR TWO: $60

T he Harvest features both a café and dining room, as well as a lush outdoor patio for pleasant summer dining. The bar is popular with young professionals and junior Harvard staff.

The menus change frequently to reflect seasonal freshness, but game and fish are always offered. The Harvest offers an extensive wine list from Italy, France and the U.S.

A typical menu might include Potato Wrapped Filet of Sole; Long Island Duckling stuffed with Pork, Liver and Dried Cranberries; Vegetarian Ravioli with Beets, Goat Cheese and Butternut Squash; Jambalaya; Hummus Platter; Grilled Leg of Lamb with Feta; and Roasted Freshwater Catfish.

THE HARVEST'S MENU FOR FOUR

Braised Rabbit with Pappardelle Noodles

Stuffed Rack of Lamb

Roasted Monkfish with Mussels in a Sambuca Cream Broth

Braised Rabbit
with Pappardelle Noodles

repare marinade by combining wine, bay leaves, peppercorns, juniper berries, allspice leaves, thyme, shallots, carrot, leek and celery.

Cut rabbit into quarters. Marinate, refrigerated, for 48 hours.

Remove the rabbit from the marinade, pat dry. Reserve marinade. Dust the rabbit with flour and season with salt and pepper.

In a sauté pan brown the rabbit in oil. Remove the rabbit from the pan and sauté the carrot, celery, leek and thyme sprigs from the marinade. Deglaze the vegetables with the strained marinade, add the rabbit and cook for 1 hour over low heat.

Remove the rabbit from the liquid and skim off any fat. Reduce the sauce to the consistency of a thick tomato sauce. Add the chocolate.

Remove meat from bones and add the meat to the sauce. Serve over pappardelle pasta.

Serves 4
Preparation Time:
  30 Minutes
(note marinating time)
Cooking Time:
  1 Hour

- 1 **bottle cabernet (red wine)**
- 2 **bay leaves**
- 6 **peppercorns**
- 6 **juniper berries**
- 6 **allspice leaves**
  Fresh thyme sprigs
- 4 **shallots, chopped**
- 1 **carrot, coarsely chopped**
- 1 **leek, coarsely chopped**
- 1 **stalk celery, coarsely chopped**
- 1 **whole rabbit**
  Flour, salt and pepper for dusting
  Vegetable oil for frying
- 2 **oz. bitter chocolate, shaved**
- 1 **lb. pappardelle pasta, cooked**

Stuffed Rack of Lamb

Serves 4
Preparation Time:
  20 Minutes
Cooking Time:
  25 Minutes

  6 **oz. goat cheese**
  1 **small garlic bulb,**
    roasted, skins removed
  1 **Tbsp. fresh rosemary,**
    minced
  1 **small red bell pepper,**
    roasted, seeded, diced
  2 **chicken breasts,**
    skinned, boned
  1 **egg white**
 ½ **cup heavy cream**
  2 **lamb racks, trimmed**

In a mixing bowl, combine the goat cheese, garlic, red pepper and rosemary. Blend well.

In a food processor, process the chicken breasts and egg white in a chilled bowl. Fold in cream a little at a time.

Combine the chicken mixture with the goat cheese mixture. Spread evenly over the lamb. Wrap each rack in foil.

Place lamb on a baking sheet and bake at 400° for 25 minutes for medium-rare.

Slice the chops apart and serve immediately.

Trade Secret: This dish is served at The Harvest with wilted spinach, new potatoes and deep fried baby artichokes.

Roasted Monkfish with Mussels in Sambuca Cream Sauce

Boil fish stock in a stockpot. Add the potatoes, tomatoes, leek, squash and zucchini. Season to taste. Add the cream, bring to a boil, then reduce heat to a simmer.

Pan sear the monkfish in hot oil to a golden brown. Place in the oven at 400° until cooked, about 15 to 20 minutes.

Add the mussels and sambuca to the fish broth. Cover and cook until mussels open, about six minutes. Season to taste.

Serve the broth with the mussels and vegetables in a deep bowl with the fish placed on top. Garnish with chopped chives.

Fish Stock

Place all ingredients in a large stock pot and add water until covered. Boil, skim, and simmer one hour.

Strain through a cheesecloth.

Serves 4
Preparation Time:
  20 Minutes
Cooking Time:
  20 Minutes

   1 cup fish stock (recipe follows)
   8 new potatoes, blanched, sliced ⅛" thick
   2 tomatoes, peeled, seeded, roughly chopped
   1 leek, julienned
   1 summer squash, diced large
   1 zucchini, diced large
   1 cup heavy cream
   4 monkfish, 6 oz. each, cleaned
     Oil for frying
  24 black mussels
   ¼ cup sambuca
     Chives, chopped, for garnish

Fish Stock:
   1 salmon or codfish carcass
  1½ cups dry white wine
   1 bay leaf
   3 peppercorns
   1 thyme sprig
   1 parsley sprig
   1 fennel bulb
   1 leek
   3 shallots

☆

JASPER'S

NEW ENGLAND SEAFOOD CUISINE
240 Commercial Street
Boston, Massachusetts
(617) 523-1126
Dinner Tuesday–Thursday 6PM–10PM,
       Friday–Saturday 6PM–10:30PM
AVERAGE DINNER FOR TWO: $90

J asper's is one of the most celebrated seafood spots in New England. Chef Jasper White has been internationally recognized for his combination of traditional dishes with a new flair. He says he seeks a "sense of delight" in his food and in his restaurant.

The decor is sleek and elegant, with the original 1802 brickwork and beams offset by modern art and glass sculpture, as well as posters from the early 1900s. Jasper's has three dining areas, the first with four deep cherrywood booths and a mahogany bar. The middle room has upper and lower areas, separated by a cherrywood and glass sideboard, which holds part of Jasper's extensive wine selection. The third revolves around the modern mobile/light, and is often used for banquets. White-clothed tables and red lacquer chairs complete the scene.

The signature dishes include Corn, Pumpkin and Leek Bisque with Lobster; a Braised Halibut; and Mussels in Lobster Broth with Mushroom and Leeks. When dessert time comes, there is likely to be a marvelous Spiced Chocolate Tweed Cake or a Lemon Puff Pastry with Plum Sauce.

JASPER'S MENU FOR FOUR

Oyster Stew

Half-Crispy Fish with Scallion Purée

Pear Upside Down Spice Cake

Oyster Stew

P ick through the oysters carefully, removing any bits of shell. Place in a small saucepan with their liquid and 2 cups water. Heat slowly until the oysters begin to curl. Remove and set aside. Strain the liquid and set aside.

In a soup pot, slowly simmer the onion and celery root in butter until tender, about 6 minutes. Add the oyster liquid and heavy cream. Heat almost to boiling and simmer for 10 minutes. Add the oysters, parsley, chervil and pepper to taste. Simmer 1 minute more.

Trade Secret: Most shellfish stews are made with milk. The advantage of heavy cream is that it almost never breaks, or curdles, the way milk does.

© "Jasper White's Cooking From New England"

Serves 4
Preparation Time:
  20 Minutes
Cooking Time:
  15 Minutes

  1 pt. shucked oysters,
    with liquid
  ½ cup onion, finely diced
  ½ cup celery root, or
    peeled celery, finely
    diced
  6 Tbsps. (¾ stick) butter,
    unsalted
1½ cups heavy cream
  2 Tbsps. fresh parsley,
    chopped
  1 Tbsp. fresh chervil,
    chopped
    Pepper to taste

Half-Crispy Fish with Scallion Purée

Serves 4
Preparation Time:
  40 Minutes

12 scallions
 6 Tbsps. (¾ stick) butter,
    unsalted
 1 Tbsp. white rice wine
    vinegar
    Salt and pepper to
    taste
    Fish stock, optional
 4 sea bass filets or ocean
    perch, 8 oz. each
 1 cup milk
 1 cup flour
    Cayenne pepper to
    taste
 ¼ cup peanut oil for
    frying

Cut the scallions in half across. Discard the roots. Cut half the green part into thin diagonal slices for garnish. Set aside sliced and unsliced green parts of the scallions.

Place the white parts in a small saucepan with 3 Tbsps. butter and 2 Tbsps. water. Simmer very slowly until tender, about 10 minutes. Add the unsliced green parts and cook for 1 minute.

Remove from heat and purée in a food processor or blender. Pass through a coarse strainer into a clean saucepan. Rewarm gently. Stir in the remaining butter. Season to taste with vinegar, salt and pepper. Adjust the consistency with a little water or fish stock so that it will spread on a plate. Keep warm.

Remove any scales or bones from the filets. Do not remove the skin. Score the skin of each filet about ¾" apart, cutting into the meat as little as possible. Carefully dip the skin side of a filet in the milk, then in the flour seasoned with salt, pepper and cayenne. Repeat each dip. Continue with remaining filets. Do not get flour on the meat of the fish.

Heat a sauté pan with ¼" peanut oil to medium heat. Put the filets in the pan, skin sides down. Cover the pan loosely with a lid or pie tin. The fish should be sizzling. Check periodically, cooking for 5 to 7 minutes.

Spread the scallion purée on each plate and place the fish, skin side up, on the purée.

© "Jasper White's Cooking From New England"

Pear Upside-Down Spice Cake

Peel and core the pears. Cut into ½" slices. Toss the pears in a hot sauté pan with 2 Tbsps. butter and the sugar until the pears are nicely browned and the sugar is caramelized. Add 2 Tbsps. water and remove from heat. Set aside.

Combine ½ cup brown sugar and 4 Tbsps. butter in an ovenproof, non-stick skillet and cook over low heat until a syrup forms. Carefully arrange the pears in a circular pattern over the syrup.

Cream 6 Tbsps. butter with 3 Tbsps. brown sugar in a mixing bowl, beating until light and fluffy. Beat in the egg yolks. Stir in the molasses.

Sift together the flour, baking soda, salt, ginger, cinnamon and nutmeg. Fold into the batter without overmixing.

Beat all six egg whites until stiff peaks form. Fold into the batter. Spread the batter evenly over the pears in the skillet.

Bake at 350° for about 25 minutes, or until the center of the cake springs back when touched.

To unmold, place a serving plate over the pan and turn it, inverting the cake onto the plate. Serve warm or at room temperature with whipped cream.

Trade Secret: Traditional pineapple rings can be substituted for pears in this recipe. Also, a 9" cake pan can be used instead of a non-stick skillet, but be careful when unmolding.

© "Jasper White's Cooking From New England"

Yield: One 9" or 10" cake
Preparation Time:
  30 Minutes
Cooking Time:
  20 Minutes

  6 Anjou or Bartlett pears
 ¾ cup (1½ sticks) butter,
    unsalted
 ⅓ cup sugar
 ½ cup + 3 Tbsps. brown
    sugar, packed
  2 eggs, separated
 ½ cup molasses
  1 cup cake flour, sifted
  1 tsp. baking soda
 ½ tsp. salt
  1 tsp. ginger, ground
  1 tsp. cinnamon, ground
  1 tsp. nutmeg, ground
  4 egg whites
    Whipped cream

JULIEN

FRENCH CUISINE
The Hotel Meridien
250 Franklin Street
Boston, Massachusetts
(617) 451-1900
Open Daily 7AM–11PM
AVERAGE DINNER FOR TWO: $85

Incomparable elegance surrounds the diner at Julien in the Hotel Meridien. Once the "Members' Court" reception room for the governors of the Federal Reserve Bank, Julien is a grand Renaissance Revival room dating back to 1922. White and gold accents gleam in the glow of the magnificent crystal chandeliers hanging in the high vaulted ceiling above. Two N.C. Wyeth murals grace the paneled walls. Julien is one of the finest French restaurants in New England, with impressive chefs and an equally impressive wine list.

Samples from the menu include Pheasant Consommé with Game-Stuffed Cabbage, Terrine of Venison, Ragout of Scallops with Truffles and Duck Foie Gras, Salmon Soufflé, Filet Mignon of Veal with Morels, Seven-Hour Braised Rabbit, and Filet of Lamb Stuffed with Spinach Mousse.

JULIEN'S MENU FOR FOUR

Lobster Soufflé

Seafood Pot au Feu

Mushrooms in Puff Pastry Shells

Lobster Soufflé

Butter and flour four 4-oz. ramekins and set them in the freezer.

Beat together the egg yolks and the truffle juice over a double boiler. Whisk the mixture until it is light and ribbony. Let cool to room temperature.

Purée the foie gras and strain through a fine sieve.

Mix the purée with the egg yolks.

Whip the egg whites with salt and cream of tartar until firm peaks form. Slowly fold together the two egg mixtures.

Place equal amounts of diced lobster in each ramekin and half fill each with the soufflé mixture. Place the ramekins in a bain marie, or in a large baking dish, with hot water halfway up the sides of the ramekins. Bake for 15 minutes, or until cooked, at 350°.

Serves 4
Preparation Time:
   20 Minutes
Cooking Time:
   15 Minutes
Pre-heat oven to 350°

   1 Tbsp. butter, unsalted
   1 Tbsp. flour
   4 eggs, separated
   ¼ cup truffle juice
   2 oz. foie gras
   ⅛ tsp. salt
   ⅛ tsp. cream of tartar
   1 lobster tail, cooked, diced

☆

Seafood Pot au Feu

Serves 4
Preparation Time:
  30 Minutes

  ¼ **cup bacon, diced**
  2 **Tbsps. butter, clarified**
  ¼ **cup celery, diced**
  ¼ **cup onion, diced**
  3 **Tbsps. flour**
  2 **cups fish stock**
  2 **cups light cream**
  4 **sea scallops**
  4 **mussels**
  4 **clams**
  4 **salmon pieces, 1 oz.**
    each
  4 **halibut pieces, 1 oz.**
    each
  4 **lobster pieces, 1 oz.**
    each
  2 **scallions, cut in**
    2" lengths
  1 **sprig thyme**
  2 **Tbsps. butter,**
    unsweetened
    Salt and pepper to
    taste

 n a large pot, render the bacon in the clarified butter. Add the celery and onion. Sauté until the onion is translucent.

Add the flour, whisk, and cook about 5 minutes. Then add the fish stock and bring to a simmer. When the fish stock starts simmering, add the cream and all the seafood, scallions and thyme.

When the clams and mussels open, remove the seafood and place it in individual soup bowls.

Whisk unsweetened butter into the pot, season with salt and pepper.

Ladle the broth over the seafood. Top with chopped parsley.

☆

Mushrooms in Puff Pastry Shells

Bake the puff pastry shells according to manufacturer's directions until golden brown. Keep warm.

In a sauté pan, melt the butter and sauté the mushrooms with garlic, salt, pepper and star anise. Add the Pernod. Remove the mushrooms when they are fully cooked. Reserve the liquid.

Add the veal stock and cream to the mushroom liquid. Reduce by half.

Open the puff pastry shells and empty out the centers. Fill with warm mushrooms. Top with warm sauce.

Serves 6
Preparation Time:
15 Minutes
Cooking Time:
15 Minutes

6 puff pastry shells
3 Tbsps. butter
½ lb. wild mushrooms
1 lb. button mushrooms
2 garlic cloves, chopped
   Salt and pepper to taste
1 star anise, chopped
2 Tbsps. Pernod
1 cup veal stock
2 cups cream
   Chives, chopped for garnish

L'ESPALIER

NEW ENGLAND CUISINE
30 Gloucester Street
Boston, Massachusetts
(617) 262-3023
Dinner Monday–Saturday 6:00PM–10PM
AVERAGE DINNER FOR TWO: $110

Located in an historic 1876 townhouse in Boston's elegant Back Bay, L'Espalier boasts a fireplace, hand-carved woodwork and striking floral arrangements. The culinary artistry of the cuisine complements their stylish setting. A native New Englander, Chef Frank McClelland's cuisine is contemporary French with a New England theme.

The menu stars such specialties as Chilled Roasted Sweet Garlic and Summer Squash Soup with Maine Lobster Salad, Grilled Squab in Raspberry Butter with White Bean and Lemon Salad, Flail of New York Foie Gras, Roasted Atlantic Striped Bass in Black Olive Crust, Grilled Young Pheasant in Garlic Crust with Chanterelles and Zucchini Potato Cake, Barbecued Filet of Beef and Chocolate Opera Cake with Blackberry Coulis.

L'ESPALIER'S MENU FOR SIX

Chanterelle Cappuccino Soup

Pecan Crusted Spring Lamb

Blood Orange Soufflé

Chanterelle Cappuccino Soup

P lace mushroom stems, onion, celery, leek, 1 shallot, and half the garlic in a large stock pot. Add water and all herbs and spices. Bring to a boil and simmer for 10 minutes. Add 1 cup wine and continue to simmer another 15 minutes. Strain. Place the liquid back into the stock pot and continue to cook until reduced by half. Reserve.

Pour 1 tsp. olive oil in a skillet with the remaining shallots, garlic and sliced mushroom heads. Cook for 4 minutes, stirring constantly. Add the Madeira and 1 cup wine and let cook for 2 minutes.

Place the mushroom mixture in a blender with the vegetable bouillon and blend. Pour back into the stock pot and add the cream. Season to taste with salt, pepper and lemon juice.

To serve, top each bowl of soup with steamed milk from a cappuccino milk steamer or scald one cup of milk, allow to cool, then add 2 egg yolks and whisk in a double boiler until it foams. Ladle onto the soup. Garnish with tarragon, parsley and/or chervil.

Serves 6
Preparation Time:
1 Hour

1½ lbs. chanterelle or
    morel mushrooms,
    heads sliced, stems
    chopped
1 onion, chopped
1 stalk celery, chopped
1 leek, chopped
3 shallots, minced
4 garlic cloves, crushed
2 qts. water
    Zest of one lemon
1 clove, whole
2 peppercorns
1 sprig parsley
1 tsp. thyme, dried
1 tsp. tarragon
2 bay leaves
2 cups white wine
2 tsps. olive oil
½ cup Madeira
⅓ cup heavy cream
    Salt and pepper to
    taste
    Lemon juice to taste
    Steamed milk
2 egg yolks, optional
    Herbs for garnish

Pecan Crusted Spring Lamb

Serves 6
Preparation Time:
  30 Minutes
(note marinating time)
Cooking Time:
  20 Minutes

  2 Tbsps. dried rosemary
  2 Tbsps. red pepper
    flakes
  ¼ cup mustard seeds
  1 Tbsp. cumin seeds,
    ground
  1 Tbsp. coriander,
    ground
  2 Tbsps. mustard,
    ground
  2 Tbsps. pepper
  ¼ cup balsamic vinegar
  1 cup olive oil
  ¼ cup fresh mint,
    chopped
    Lamb rack or loin
  1 cup cornmeal
1½ cups chicken stock
  ¾ cup pecans, roasted
  ¼ cup garlic paste
  1 cup molasses
    Salt and pepper to
    taste
    Whole grain mustard
  ¼ cup flour

I n a mixing bowl combine the rosemary, pepper flakes, mustard seeds, cumin, coriander, ground mustard, pepper, balsamic vinegar, olive oil and mint. Toss with the lamb and let marinate overnight in the refrigerator.

Roast cornmeal in the oven at 400° until light brown, about 7 minutes. In a large pot, bring the chicken stock to a boil. Add the cornmeal slowly, stirring constantly. Cook for 15 minutes. Remove from pot and pour into a blender. Add the pecans, garlic paste, and molasses. Add the salt, pepper and whole grain mustard to taste. Purée until smooth.

Salt and sear the marinated lamb in a hot skillet. Dust lamb with flour and spread a thin layer of the pecan mixture on top.

Place lamb on a roasting rack in the oven at 425°. Cook for 17 to 20 minutes for medium rare, or to desired doneness.

Blood Orange Soufflé

Place orange juice in a saucepan over medium heat until reduced to ¾ cup.

In a separate stockpot, melt the butter. Add the flour and cook for 2 minutes on low heat. Add the milk and whisk in the orange liqueur. Add the vanilla bean and the sugar, reserving 1 Tbsp. of the sugar. Cook until thick and then an additional 5 minutes more. Add the orange juice. Remove from heat and cool to room temperature. Add the egg yolks and orange zest.

Whip the egg whites to soft peaks, then stir in the arrowroot or cornstarch and 1 Tbsp. sugar. Fold the whites into the soufflé.

Pour into individual soufflé dishes that have been lightly buttered and sugared. Bake for 15 to 20 minutes at 400°.

Serves 6
Preparation Time:
  20 Minutes
Baking Time:
  20 Minutes

  2 cups orange juice
    (preferably from blood
    oranges)
  2 Tbsps. butter
  4 Tbsps. all-purpose
    flour
  1 cup whole milk
  1 Tbsp. orange liqueur
  1 vanilla bean, split
    lengthwise
  ½ cup sugar
  4 egg yolks
    Zest of two oranges
  6 egg whites
  ⅛ tsp. arrowroot or
    cornstarch

☆

MICHELA'S

ITALIAN CUISINE
One Athenaeum Street
Cambridge, Massachusetts
(617) 225-2121
Dinner Sunday–Thursday 6:00PM–10PM
         Friday–Saturday 6:00PM–10:30PM
AVERAGE DINNER FOR TWO: $50

L ocated in the historic Carter Ink Building in Kendall Square, Cambridge, Michela's offers a choice of dining experiences. The Dining Room is stylish, elegant and vibrant in its palette of colors. Warm yellow ochres and earthy Tuscan red harmonize with a scenic wall mural that provides the backdrop for the crisp, white linens decorated with Michela's signature breadsticks and a bright red pepper grinder. The enclosed atrium just out-side the dining room is known as Café M. An oasis in the building, the atrium is filled with lush greenery and brightly colored umbrellas.

Star chef Jody Adams changes the menu every eight weeks, highlighting seasonal foods and different regions of Italy with each change. Michela's also offers an extensive international wine list to complement the changing menus. Samples from the antipasto selections include Buffalo Mozzarella, Rolled Sausage & Eggplant "Stroller," Baby Artichokes with Fritters and Zucchini Blossoms and Veal, Rabbit and Hazelnut Terrine. Entrées run the gamut from Three Little Pizzas from the Sea, Corn Cake and Salt Cod Torta, Risotto with Veal Meatballs, Roasted Bass Wrapped in Greens, Marinated Long Island Duck to Seared Tuna Steak with Tomato Bruschetta.

MICHELA'S MENU FOR FOUR

Roasted Pear Radicchio Salad in Balsamic Vinaigrette

Ravioli Stuffed with Mushrooms, Garlic, and Potatoes

Brodetto of Bass with Tomatoes and Pasta

Seared Quail on Polenta

with Raisins, Pine Nuts, Pomegranates and Sage

very good [handwritten]

Roasted Pear and Radicchio Salad with Toasted Walnuts & Balsamic Vinaigrette

T oss the pear halves and radicchio quarters in olive oil and season with salt and pepper. Place the pears and radicchio, sliced side down, in a roasting pan. Roast in the oven for 10 to 15 minutes at 450°. *Sm. Amt. of oil goes a long way.* [handwritten]

Remove the radicchio from the oven. It should be crispy. Continue to cook the pears until they are tender and golden-brown.

To serve, toss the warm pears and radicchio in a bowl with balsamic vinegar and olive oil. Arrange on four plates. Place a piece of gorgonzola on each plate. Just before serving, warm the plates in the oven for 4 minutes or until the cheese just begins to melt.

Toss the watercress and shallots in a bowl with balsamic vinegar, olive oil, salt and pepper. Place a mound of watercress in the center of each plate and garnish with hazelnuts.

Trade Secret: For a richer dish, reduce the cream by one fourth. Whisk in the gorgonzola until smooth. Salt and pepper to taste. Put a spoonful of gorgonzola sauce on a warm plate. Arrange the pear and radicchio on the plate.

Serves 4
Preparation Time:
30 Minutes

- 2 pears, cut in half *spatters if too much* [handwritten] *smoke!* [handwritten]
- 1 head radicchio lettuce, quartered
  Olive oil
  Salt and pepper to taste
  Balsamic vinegar
- 4 oz. gorgonzola cheese *or goat* [handwritten]
- ½ cup heavy cream, optional
- 1 bunch watercress, stems trimmed, washed, dried
- 1 shallot, peeled, sliced thin
- ½ cup toasted hazelnuts, chopped *Used walnuts* [handwritten]

Ravioli Stuffed with Mushrooms, Garlic and Potatoes

Serves 4
Preparation Time:
1 Hour

1 potato
¼ cup mascarpone
   cheese
   Salt and pepper to
   taste
8 garlic cloves, unpeeled
4 shallots
½ cup (1 stick) unsalted
   butter
1 cup mixed wild
   mushrooms, finely
   chopped
1 Tbsp. parsley, chopped
1 tsp. thyme, chopped
9 eggs
16 pasta sheets, 4"×4", for
   ravioli
   Truffle oil or browned
   butter
¼ cup Parmesan cheese,
   grated
8 sprigs parsley

Peel the potato and cut into 6 pieces. Place in a small pot and cover with water. Add a pinch of salt and cook until tender. Drain and push through a ricer while still warm. Beat in the mascarpone cheese. Season with salt and pepper.

Blanch garlic in salted water and cook until tender. Drain, cool, peel and coarsely mash. Add to the potatoes.

Finely chop one shallot. Heat 4 Tbsps. butter and cook the chopped shallot until translucent. Add the chopped mushrooms and cook until the mushrooms have released all their juices and the juices have been reduced. The mushrooms should be dry. Season with salt and pepper. Mix the mushrooms with the potato mixture. Add the parsley and thyme. Allow to cool.

Slice the remaining shallots in ⅛" slices. Heat the remaining butter in a small pan. When the foam subsides, add the shallots and cook until crispy. Keep warm. Save the butter for ravioli sauce.

Beat 1 egg with 2 Tbsps. water for egg wash. Brush the edges of a pasta sheet with the egg wash. Place 2 Tbsps. of the mushroom mixture in the center of the pasta. Make a well in the mixture. Crack an egg into a teacup. Pour the yolk and half of the white into the well. Cover with a second pasta sheet and push out as much of the air as possible. Seal the edges well. Place on a flour-dusted tea cloth. Repeat with remaining pastas.

Bring 5 qts. of water to a boil. Season with salt. Slip the ravioli into the water. Cook, stirring gently several times, for 5 minutes. Scoop out with a slotted spoon, drain, and place one on each plate. Drizzle with truffle oil or browned butter. Arrange the crisped shallots on top of each ravioli. Sprinkle with Parmesan cheese and garnish the plate with parsley.

★

Brodetto of Bass with Tomatoes

Wash the tomatoes and cut in half lengthwise. Place them in a roasting pan in a single layer. Add 6 cloves chopped garlic, basil leaves, 1 tsp. salt, ⅛ tsp. pepper flakes and sugar. Toss well. Add enough oil to cover the tomatoes. Toss well. Roast 3 hours at 250° or until tomatoes are tender, but not falling apart.

Rinse the cavities of the fish and cut diamond shaped gashes on both sides.

Mix the lemon zest, scallions, and 1 Tbsp. chopped garlic. Rub mixture into the gashes in the fish and let marinate 3 hours.

Season the fish with salt and pepper and dust with flour. Heat four large sauté pans with ⅛″ olive oil each. Sear the fish on all sides. Distribute the onions and fennel among the four fish pans and cook until tender. Add 1 more Tbsp. garlic and thyme. Deglaze each pan with 1 Tbsp. vinegar. Add 4 tomato halves, a bay leaf, a pinch of pepper flakes and ½ cup water to each pan.

Place the pans in the oven and roast at 350° for 15 minutes or until done.

Serves 4
Preparation Time:
 40 Minutes
(note marinating time)
Cooking Time:
 3 Hours, 15 Minutes

24 **plum tomatoes**
 6 **cloves + 2 Tbsps. garlic, chopped**
18 **basil leaves**
 1 **tsp. salt**
⅛ **tsp. hot red pepper flakes**
⅛ **tsp. sugar**
   Olive oil
 4 **whole bass, 1 lb. each**
   Zest of 2 lemons
 2 **scallions, chopped**
   Salt and pepper to taste
   Flour
 1 **cup onions, diced**
 1 **cup fennel, diced**
 4 **sprigs fresh thyme**
 4 **Tbsps. white wine vinegar**
 4 **bay leaves**

☆

Seared Quail on Polenta with Raisins, Pine Nuts, Pomegranates & Sage

Serves 4
Preparation Time:
 40 Minutes
(note marinating time)
Cooking Time:
 40 Minutes

 8 whole quail, boned
 2 shallots, thinly sliced
16 sage leaves, chopped
 1 tsp. pepper
   Olive oil
   Salt and pepper to
   taste
¼ cup shallots, minced
 2 Tbsps. garlic, chopped
 1 cup Marsala wine
 2 cups chicken stock
 1 Tbsp. balsamic vinegar
¼ cup pomegranate
   seeds
 2 Tbsps. pine nuts
 2 Tbsps. raisins, steeped
   in water just to cover
¼ lb. spinach leaves,
   cleaned

Polenta recipe follows
on page 121.

Toss the quail with the 2 sliced shallots, half of the chopped sage, 1 tsp. pepper and enough oil to coat the birds. Marinate in the refrigerator for 3 hours.

Heat 2 large frying pans with ⅛" olive oil in each. Season the birds with salt. Sear about 5 minutes per side, until brown and cooked through. Set aside and keep warm. Add 2 Tbsps. minced shallots and 1 Tbsp. garlic to one of the pans, with more oil if necessary. Cook for 3 minutes. Deglaze the pan with the Marsala and reduce to a glaze. Add the stock and reduce by ⅔. Add the vinegar, remaining sage and pomegranate seeds. Season with salt and pepper. Keep warm.

Add the remaining shallots and garlic with the pine nuts to the second pan. Cook until the nuts are golden and the shallots are tender. Add the raisins and the spinach, salt and pepper, and cook until the spinach is just wilted.

To serve, place a large spoonful of polenta (recipe follows) in the center of each serving plate. Arrange the spinach on top, set two quail on the spinach and spoon the sauce over the birds.

Polenta

Bring the water and salt to a boil in a large saucepan. Mix the cornmeal with the remaining water and add to the boiling water in a steady stream.

Whisk constantly until the polenta comes to a boil. Reduce heat and cook, stirring occasionally, for 40 minutes or until mixture is smooth and shiny.

Add the cheese and butter. Salt and pepper to taste. Keep warm.

Serves 4
Preparation Time:
  5 Minutes
Cooking Time:
  40 Minutes

  4 **cups water**
    Salt to taste
  1 **cup cornmeal**
  ¼ **cup Parmesan cheese,**
    grated
  2 **Tbsps. unsalted butter**

OLIVES

MEDITERRANEAN CUISINE
10 City Square
Charlestown, Massachusetts
(617) 242-1999
Dinner Monday–Friday 5:30PM–10:30PM,
      Saturday–Sunday 5PM–10:30PM
AVERAGE DINNER FOR TWO: $65

O lives has become the place to see and be seen in Boston. Loyal patrons line up hours before the nightly opening, as the hot spot only takes reservations for parties of six or more. Chef/owner Todd English has transformed the 200-year-old former dance hall into a scene awhirl with waiters and cooks bustling to feed the throngs. Yet a sense of elegance remains amid large century-old paned windows, fresh flowers and a mahogany bar.

English also owns the less formal Figs in Charlestown, featuring specialty pizzas, and his newest venture, Isola (co-owned with Michael J. Fox, Glenn Close and Cam Neely) in Martha's Vineyard.

Some of the mouth-watering options from Olives are Pan-Braised Shrimp in Buttery Champagne Broth on Truffle Mashed Potatoes; Tuna Carpaccio on Flatbread with Mesclun Greens and Herbs; Tart of Olives, Goat Cheese, Onion and Anchovies; Porcini Ravioli on Confit of Chicken Ragu; Spit Roasted Herb and Garlic Basted Chicken on Mashed Potato Cake with Garlic, Basil, Onions and Green Beans; and Falling Chocolate Cake with Raspberry Sauce.

OLIVES' MENU FOR SIX

Roasted Oysters

Roasted Red Pepper Salad

Marinated Lamb Sandwich with Spicy Aioli

Risotto with Wild Mushrooms and Asparagus

Roasted Oysters

In a medium bowl, combine the lemon juice, vinegar, mascarpone and sour cream until blended.

Fold in the radicchio and scallions. Season with salt and pepper.

Line a baking dish with rock salt and seaweed.

Place a heaping tablespoon of mascarpone mixture into each oyster. Set oysters snugly in the rock salt.

Broil until done, 3 to 4 minutes, 3" from the heat.

Serves 6
Preparation Time:
  30 Minutes
Pre-heat broiler

24 oysters, shucked
  Juice and zest of 1
  lemon
1 Tbsp. balsamic vinegar
1 cup mascarpone
  cheese
2 Tbsps. sour cream
1 head radicchio,
  shredded
5 scallions, cut
  lengthwise
1 Tbsp. fresh thyme,
  roughly chopped
  Salt and pepper to
  taste
  Rock salt
  Seaweed, blanched

Marinated Lamb Sandwich

Serves 6
Preparation Time:
  15 Minutes
(note refrigeration time)
Cooking Time:
  25 Minutes

  1 **leg of lamb, 6 lbs.,**
     butterflied
  1 **recipe lamb marinade,**
     recipe follows
  6 **slices of bread,**
     ¾" thick

Lamb marinade:
  ½ **cup paprika**
  4 **Tbsps. cumin**
  4 **Tbsps. fresh rosemary**
  1 **tsp. cayenne pepper**
  2 **Tbsps. turmeric**
  ½ **tsp. cinnamon**
  ¼ **tsp. nutmeg**
  8 **garlic cloves**
  1 **cup olive oil**

F or the marinade: Combine all the marinade ingredients except the olive oil in a food processor. Pulse a few times to roughly chop the herbs. Add the olive oil and purée.

Trim any excess fat from the leg of lamb. Cover the entire leg with the marinade, reserving ½ cup. Place lamb in a shallow dish, cover and refrigerate at least 3 hours or up to 48 hours.

Grill lamb 12 to 15 minutes on each side. Remove from heat and let stand 5 to 10 minutes.

Toast bread on the grill until brown, 2 to 3 minutes each side.

Slice lamb thinly and pile slices on top of each piece of toast. Drizzle with 2 Tbsps. marinade.

Trade Secret: Save remaining marinade for other uses: see Spicy Aioli and Roasted Red Pepper Salad, following pages.

Spicy Aioli

P lace the red peppers on a grill or under a broiler until skins are blackened. Remove the skins and seeds.
Place the garlic, marinade and lemon juice in a food processor and purée. Add the red peppers and egg yolks and purée. While the machine is running, add the olive oil in a thin stream. Process until the mixture is thick and creamy. Add water to thin if necessary. Salt and pepper to taste.

Serves 6
Preparation Time:
15 Minutes

3 red bell peppers
1 large garlic clove, peeled
4 Tbsps. lamb marinade, see page 124
4 tsps. lemon juice
2 egg yolks
1 cup olive oil
5 Tbsps. water
Salt and pepper to taste

☆

Roasted Red Pepper Salad

Serves 6
Preparation Time:
  20 Minutes

  6 large red bell peppers
  1 large red onion, thinly
    sliced
  3 scallions, finely
    chopped
  3 Tbsps. lemon juice
  2 Tbsps. lemon zest
  2 Tbsps. lamb marinade,
    see recipe page 124
  ½ cup olive oil
  1 lb. salad greens

P lace the red peppers on a grill or under a broiler until the skins are blackened. Place in a bowl and cover with plastic wrap until peppers are cool enough to handle. Remove the skins and seeds then julienne.

In a separate bowl, mix the peppers with the remaining ingredients except the greens.

Toss with the greens and serve.

★

Risotto with Wild Mushrooms and Asparagus

Boil 4 cups water and blanch asparagus until bright green.

Cut off the top 2" of each asparagus spear and set aside.

In a food processor, purée the remaining asparagus stems with 1 cup of stock.

In a large saucepan, melt half the butter over medium heat. Sauté the mushrooms and onions. Add rice and stir to coat. Deglaze with wine, then bring to a boil.

Add one cup of stock at a time, stirring until rice absorbs liquid. Continue adding the stock until the rice is cooked.

Stir in remaining butter and Parmesan. Season to taste and garnish with parsley.

Serves 6
Preparation Time:
30 Minutes

- 1 bunch asparagus, peeled
- 6 to 8 cups beef or veal stock
- ¼ cup (½ stick) butter
- 2 cups button mushrooms, thinly sliced
- 2 cups wild mushrooms, thinly sliced
- 1 large onion, finely chopped
- 2½ cups arborio short-grain rice
- 1 cup dry white wine
- ½ cup Parmesan cheese, grated
  Salt and pepper to taste
- ½ bunch Italian parsley, chopped

★

SEASONS

NEW AMERICAN CUISINE
The Bostonian Hotel at
Faneuil Hall Marketplace
Boston, Massachusetts
(617) 523-9970
Dinner Monday–Sunday 6PM–10PM
AVERAGE DINNER FOR TWO: $70

Enclosed in glass, the multi-level restaurant at The Bostonian Hotel puts diners in the heart of historic Boston. Fresh flowers and plants, subtle grays and greens, and crisp white tablecloths create an airy, open atmosphere in any season. The lighted stainless steel ceiling and arched wooden beams continue the sense of spaciousness.

In addition to its highly rated food, Seasons offers an extensive and exclusively American wine list. Samples from the Seasons menu include Crab and Sweet Potato Tamale, Lobster and Sweet Corn Chowder, Three Bean Cassoulet with Duck Confit and Sausage, Juniper Rubbed Roast Venison with Sweet Potato Spoonbread and Dry Cherries and Hot Chocolate Truffle Soufflé with Tia Maria Ice Cream.

SEASONS' MENU FOR SIX

Roasted Pumpkin Soup

Charred Squid and Asparagus Salad

Pan Seared Trout with Bruised Olives

Roasted Pumpkin Soup

Trim the skins and remove the seeds from the pumpkins. Cut the pumpkin meat into 2" chunks. Toss the pumpkin chunks with ¼ cup oil, salt and pepper.

Place the pumpkin chunks in a single layer on a baking sheet and bake in the oven until just brown around the edges, about 15 minutes.

Pour ¼ cup oil into a large pot on medium heat. Add the onions and cook about 3 minutes or until lightly browned. Add the garlic and cook for 5 minutes more. Add the pumpkin, chicken stock and spices to the pot. Simmer 30 to 40 minutes or until the pumpkin is very soft.

Purée the soup in a food processor. Adjust the consistency with the chicken stock. Season to taste.

For the garnish, in a mixing bowl combine the pumpkin seeds, 1 Tbsp. vegetable oil, salt and pepper to taste and sugar. Bake at 425° for 5 to 7 minutes or until the seeds are toasted. Sprinkle seeds on top of each bowl of soup before serving.

Serves 6
Preparation Time:
  30 Minutes
Cooking Time:
  30 Minutes
Pre-heat oven to 425°

  2 **medium pumpkins**
  ½ **cup + 1 Tbsp. vegetable oil**
    Salt and pepper to taste
  2 **large yellow onions, julienned**
  5 **garlic cloves, minced**
  3 to 5 **qts. chicken stock**
  1½ **tsps. cumin, ground**
  1 **Tbsp. coriander, ground**
  2 **bay leaves**
  ½ **cup dry pumpkin seeds**
  ½ **tsp. sugar.**

☆

Charred Squid and Asparagus Salad

Serves 6
Preparation Time:
30 Minutes

¼ cup olive oil
1 lb. squid, cleaned, cut
   into rings
1 lb. asparagus,
   trimmed, cut into
   1" pieces
   Juice of 1 lemon
⅛ tsp. sugar
⅛ tsp. salt
⅛ tsp. crushed red
   pepper
2 oz. feta cheese,
   crumbled
1 Tbsp. Italian parsley,
   chopped
   Salt and pepper to
   taste

In a large skillet, heat 1 Tbsp. of the olive oil until it begins to smoke.

Season the squid with sugar, salt and red pepper. Add the squid to the hot oil. Cook for 2 minutes, stirring often. Squeeze half the lemon over the squid. Remove the squid, place in a large bowl, and set aside.

Repeat this process with the asparagus pieces.

In a mixing bowl, combine the squid, asparagus, feta cheese, chopped parsley and remaining olive oil. Season to taste.

Serve warm or chilled.

★

Pan Seared Trout with Braised Olives

I n a medium saucepan, heat the olive oil over medium heat. Add the onions and garlic. Cook until tender, stirring often. Add the tomatoes, raisins and olives. Cook 5 minutes. Add the stocks and simmer for 30 minutes. Add the lemon juice, chopped herbs, salt and pepper. Simmer 10 minutes more. Set sauce aside.

Combine the flour with salt and pepper to taste. Set aside.

Cook the bacon strips, reserving the fat.

Dredge the trout in the flour mixture.

Heat 2 Tbsps. of the bacon fat in a skillet until it begins to smoke. Place one trout in the skillet, skin side up. Cook 1½ minutes on each side. Repeat with remaining trout.

Place trout, skin side up, on a cutting board. With a knife, remove the center strip of fins and bones, leaving two filets.

To serve, place two filets on each plate and top with the braised olive sauce and strips of cooked bacon.

Serves 6
Preparation Time:
  30 Minutes
Cooking Time:
  45 Minutes

  1 Tbsp. olive oil
  1 yellow onion, diced
  2 garlic cloves, minced
  2 tomatoes, peeled, seeded, diced
  ¼ cup raisins
  ½ cup Kalamata olives, seeded, quartered
  ½ cup green Spanish olives, seeded, sliced
  2½ cups fish stock
  2½ cups chicken stock
     Juice of ½ lemon
  2 tsps. thyme, chopped
  2 tsps. Italian parsley, chopped
     Salt and pepper to taste
  1 cup flour
  12 strips bacon
  6 trout, bones, heads, tails removed

THE CHANTICLEER

FRENCH CUISINE
9 New Street
Siasconset, Nantucket, Massachusetts
(508) 257-6231
Lunch Noon–2:30PM
Dinner 6:30PM–12:30AM
AVERAGE DINNER FOR TWO: $120

Within this rose-covered cottage is one of the island's finest restaurants. Lunch in the rose garden is a local tradition, as is an after-dinner drink in the bar. Both a five-course prix-fixe menu and a la carte menu are available at dinner. The extraordinary wine cellar, which has won the Wine Spectator Grand Award, offers 900 selections of California and French wines.

For two decades, chef/owner Jean-Charles Berruet has created elegant classic-French feasts, prepared like nothing else you've ever experienced. Using fresh local ingredients and herbs, his characteristic dishes include an appetizer of Escargot and Hazelnut-filled Raviolis, served in a Sweet Garlic Broth followed by Scaloppini of Salmon sauté with a Dry Vermouth, Sorrel and Cream Sauce, or an entree of Baby Chicken stuffed with Mushrooms, Herbs and Ricotta, roasted and served with a mild Vinegar Sauce and Wild Rice Risotto. Tempting desserts range from very thin slices of Granny Smith Apples on a thin layer of Puff Pastry, cooked to order, an assortment of fresh sorbets or Chocolate Decadence served with an Espresso Sauce.

Dining at The Chanticleer is like being a privileged guest in the finest private home.

THE CHANTICLEER'S MENU FOR FOUR

Cream of Asparagus Soup

Chicken Stuffed with Herbs

in a Mild Vinegar Sauce

Chocolate Decadence with Espresso Sauce

Cream of Asparagus Soup

O pen the oysters, save and strain the liquid. Set aside. Clean the asparagus and cut 2″ off each bottom. Cut the tips off the asparagus, setting aside the base. Cook the asparagus tips in boiling water or steam, making sure to leave the asparagus slightly crisp. Remove from heat and cool.

In a large heavy soup pot, combine the milk and water, bring to a boil. Chop the remaining asparagus stems and cook them in the milk until tender.

Purée the asparagus stem mixture in a blender or food processor until smooth. Strain into another pot, add the cream, bring to a boil, add the butter, then thicken with corn starch.

Bring the oyster liquid to a boil. Cook the oysters for one minute, remove the oysters from the broth and add the broth to the soup. Season with white pepper and nutmeg; salt may not be needed.

To serve, fill each soup bowl and garnish with warm asparagus spears and oysters.

Serves 4
Preparation Time:
  1 Hour

24 **oysters**
 2 **bunches asparagus**
 1 **qt. milk**
 1 **cup water**
½ **cup cream**
 4 **Tbsps. (½ stick)**
   unsalted butter
 2 **tsps. corn starch**
   White pepper to taste
   Nutmeg to taste

Chicken Stuffed With Herbs In a Mild Vinegar Sauce

Serves 4
Preparation Time:
  30 Minutes

  4 baby chickens or game
    hens, about 1 lb. each
  2 Tbsps. unsalted butter
  ½ lb. pancetta
    Juice of 1 lemon
  1 Tbsp. water
  4 Tbsps. parsley,
    chopped
  1 Tbsp. chives, chopped
  1 tsp. tarragon, chopped
  ½ lb. mushrooms
  1 cup ricotta cheese
  4 shallots, chopped
  1 Tbsp. red wine vinegar
  ½ cup chicken stock
  3 Tbsps. heavy cream
  1 small tomato, peeled,
    seeded, chopped fine
  1 tsp. chervil, optional

In a food processor, process together the butter, pancetta, lemon juice and water for one minute. Add the parsley, chives, tarragon, mushrooms, ricotta, and 3 of the shallots. Process until mixture has the consistency of a paste.

Take each chicken and, starting from the neck side, very carefully lift the skin from the body with your fingers. Make sure you don't puncture the skin or remove it completely. Take some stuffing and carefully push it in the space between the skin and the flesh. Pay special attention to the breast and the legs.

Place the birds in a roasting pan. Cook for 10 minutes in the oven at 400° and then for 25 minutes at 350°.

Remove the chicken from the pan and discard any fat. Add the last shallot and cook for one minute. Deglaze the pan with vinegar and reduce. Add the chicken stock and the cream. Bring to a boil and allow the sauce to cook for a minute or two. Add the tomato and chervil.

Trade Secret: A wild rice risotto or fresh pasta makes a wonderful accompaniment.

Chocolate Decadence in Espresso Sauce

I n a double boiler over low heat, melt the chocolate. Remove from heat.

In a large mixing bowl, combine 7 egg yolks and 1¼ cups sugar, whipping together until fluffy. Slowly incorporate the melted chocolate, gently lifting up the mixture with a wooden spatula to make it light and airy.

In a separate bowl, work the butter with a fork, until soft and smooth. Add the cocoa powder, a small amount at a time, until well blended. Add the cocoa butter to the chocolate. Fold in the whipped cream and blend thoroughly. Set aside in a cool place.

Soak the ladyfingers in cold espresso. Line the bottom and sides of a terrine mold with parchment paper then with the ladyfingers. Fill the mold with the chocolate mix. Refrigerate overnight.

To make the espresso sauce, bring ¼ cup sugar and 2 cups milk to a boil over high heat, add the espresso grounds, cover the pot and let brew for 15 minutes.

Whisk 6 egg yolks and ¼ cups sugar in a bowl; whip until fluffy. Add the coffee infusion, mix well, and cook over low heat until the mixture has thickened slightly and coats the back of a metal spoon. Do not allow the sauce to boil or it will curdle.

Serve warm or at room temperature over the Chocolate Decadence.

Serves 4
Preparation Time:
  1 Hour
(note refrigeration time)

  5 oz. semi-sweet
    chocolate
 13 egg yolks
 1¾ cups sugar
 16 Tbsps. (2 sticks)
    unsalted butter
  ¾ cup cocoa powder
  1 cup cream, whipped
 24 ladyfingers
  1 cup espresso coffee,
    cold
  2 cups milk
  2 tsps. ground espresso

CHILLINGSWORTH

FRENCH AMERICAN CUISINE
Route 6A
Brewster, Massachusetts
(508) 896-3640
Dinner seating Tuesday–Sunday, 6:00PM, 6:30PM, 9:00PM,9:30PM
Greenhouse Bar Tuesday–Sunday, 11:30AM–2:00PM
AVERAGE DINNER FOR TWO: $135-$160

Pairing classic French training with cutting-edge nouvelle cuisine, Robert (Nitzy) Rabin and his wife, Pat, a pastry expert, create award-winning dishes at Chillingsworth. The Rabins have been serving their innovative meals for more than 17 years at the three-century-old mansion in Brewster.

Guests dine by candlelight in any one of the five dining rooms at the restaurant. Each room is decorated in Louis XV antiques and reproductions and the restaurant has working fireplaces. A harpist gently plays in the background while guests dine.

The menu is composed by Chef Rabin daily and is a five-course prix fixe meal featuring such entrées as Venison with Celery Root Purée and Fried Pumpkin, or Grilled Poussin served with Raspberry Sauce and accompanied by fresh vegetables. A stunning entrée is the Grilled Loin of Veal with Saffron Rissotto, Garlic Custard and Wild Mushroom Sauce. As appetizers, fried mussels on top of a bed of mustard sauce and tiny cakes of crab and crayfish with a spicy, but mild, saffron sauce are two tempting choices.

Pat's creations — a flourless chocolate cake with English cream, or a Mango Crème Brûlée with Fresh Raspberries — are just two of the pastry expert's delicious finales.

CHILLINGSWORTH'S MENU FOR FOUR

Oysters and Spinach in Puff Pastry

Two Melon Soup with Champagne and Mint

Lobster with Spinach, French Beans & Basil in Cognac Cream

Oysters and Spinach in a Puff Pastry

Remove the oysters from their shells by placing the oyster on a towel in the palm of your hand. Insert the tip of a knife between the shells and work the knife back and forth to carefully pry the shells apart. Cut from underneath to free the oyster from the shell. Set the oysters aside.

To prepare the sauce, combine the egg, lemon juice, and a pinch of salt and pepper in a food processor. With the processor running, slowly add the melted butter. When the butter has emulsified, stop the processor and taste for seasoning. Adjust salt and pepper and add more lemon juice to taste. Don't forget that the salmon roe may be slightly salty when it is added. Hold the sauce in a bain marie over low heat, about 155°.

Gently poach the oysters in water and white wine.

While the oysters are poaching, sauté the spinach at a high temperature, adding a small amount of whole unsalted butter, some salt and pepper and a sprinkle of water.

Place the sautéed spinach in the bottom half of each pastry, add the heated asparagus spears, cover the spinach and the asparagus stems with the poached oysters.

In a separate bowl, mix the sauce with the minced chives and the salmon roe. Drizzle the sauce over the oysters. Place the puff pastry top over the oysters and serve.

Serves 4
Preparation Time:
 45 Minutes

20 oysters
 1 egg
 ¼ cup fresh lemon juice
  Salt and pepper
 1 cup (2 sticks) unsalted
  butter, melted
 ¼ cup white wine
 1 bunch spinach,
  cleaned
 4 thin asparagus spears,
  cut to 4½", blanched
  al dente
 3 Tbsps. chives, finely
  minced
 4 tsps. salmon roe
 4 puff pastries, 2½"×4",
  baked in advance

★

Two Melon Soup
with Champagne and Mint

Serves 4
Preparation Time:
  30 Minutes

  1 **medium cantaloupe**
  1 **medium honeydew**
  1 **cup champagne**
  2 **cups fresh orange juice**
  ¼ **cup fresh lime juice**
  1 **Tbsp. honey**
  ½ **cup heavy cream,**
     whipped
     Fresh mint leaves

P eel and seed each melon. Cut melons in half. Mince one half of each melon and cut the other half into bite-size pieces.

Combine the larger pieces of melons with the orange juice, lime juice and honey, blending thoroughly. Add the minced melons and champagne to taste.

To serve, ladle the fruit into individual serving bowls and top with unsweetened whipped cream and fresh mint leaves as garnish.

Lobster with a Basil Cognac Cream

P oach or steam the lobsters until they are medium-rare, about 3 to 4 minutes. Cool and remove the meat from the shells, utilizing the two claws, the tail cut lengthwise. Save the knuckle meat and other lobster scraps, including the roe, for the sauce.

Place the lobster in a buttered baking dish. Add salt, pepper and white wine. Cover with parchment paper. Place in a warm oven for 6 to 8 minutes. The meat should "steam bake" until just hot, not overcooked.

In a sauté pan, melt the butter over medium heat. Add the reserved lobster meat and cognac. Add the stock or white veal glaze and reduce. Add the heavy cream and bring to a boil. Add the chopped basil. Taste and adjust seasonings if necessary. Strain and place the sauce aside in bain marie if it won't be served immediately.

To serve, drape the basil cognac cream over the lobster.

Serves 4
Preparation Time:
1 Hour
Pre-heat oven to 350°

- 4 **lobsters, 1½ lbs. each**
  Salt and pepper
- ½ **cup white wine**
- 4 **Tbsps. butter**
- ½ **cup cognac**
- 12 **large basil leaves,**
  chopped
- ½ **cup heavy cream**
  Chicken stock or white
  veal glaze

☆

CHRISTIAN'S RESTAURANT

CLASSIC NEW ENGLAND CUISINE
443 Main Street
Chatham, Massachusetts
(508) 945-3362
Lunch and Dinner 11:30AM–1AM
AVERAGE DINNER FOR TWO: $30

At Christian's, chef and owner Christian Schultz offers guests creative cuisine in a quaint and comfortable Cape-style setting. The downstairs dining room is decorated with old paintings, lace-covered tables, dark wood floors with Oriental runners, and Early-American print wallpaper.

A library bar, located upstairs, offers a comfortable place for guests to enjoy a cocktail and meal inside, or outside on the patio. The dark mahogany panels, old estate furniture and a bookshelf running along the ceiling give the room a homey and study-like feel.

Upstairs, guests can enjoy a menu divided into cinema theme sections. Previews include such items as Great Balls of Fire, which are fiery crab and corn fritters served with a salsa sour cream, or La Dolce Vita, an antipasto plate filled with marinated and chilled vegetables, meats and cheeses served with toasted herb bread. Burgers named The Cagney and The Bogart are oversized grilled burgers served with onions, lettuce, tomatoes, fries and a plethora of toppings suggested by the star's name.

Dinner downstairs at Christian's is a more formal affair and is highlighted by such entrées as Seafood Jambalaya. This dish is made of lobster, shrimp and scallops simmered to perfection with mushrooms and scallions in a spicy tomato sauce served over rice and garnished with more fruits of the sea, mussels and clams. A crispy Roast Duck served with Ginger Peach Sauce, and fresh pasta tossed with olive oil and lemon pepper are just two more of the many delicious selections.

For appetizers, the raw bar serves littlenecks on the half shell, oysters and shrimp cocktails. Yukae, a Japanese appetizer, is a steak tartare, tossed with pine nuts and ponzu sauce and is served with fried wontons.

CHRISTIAN'S RESTAURANT'S MENU FOR EIGHT

Fresh Maine Crabcakes

Roast Duck with Pear and Avocado Sauce

Coconut Rum Caramel Custard with Roasted Banana Sauce

Maine Crabcakes

Mix all ingredients together in a bowl. Form the crab mixture into 2-oz. patties.

Heat butter in a medium-size skillet and cook the crab cakes over medium heat until golden on both sides, about 3 minutes per side.

Serve hot with lemon wedges.

Serves 8
Preparation Time:
30 Minutes

1½ lbs. crab
  1 Tbsp. red pepper, finely diced
  1 Tbsp. green pepper, finely diced
  1 Tbsp. yellow pepper, finely diced
  1 Tbsp. parsley, finely diced
  3 Tbsps. onion, diced, sautéed
  ½ cup seasoned bread crumbs
  ½ cup Parmesan cheese
  1 whole egg
  6 drops of Tabasco sauce
  2 tsps. lemon juice
  1 Tbsp. mayonnaise
    Butter for sautéing
    Lemon wedges

✩

Roast Duck with Pear and Avocado Sauce

Serves 8
Preparation Time:
  2 Hours
Pre-heat oven to 450°

  4 ducks, approximately
    5 lbs. each
    Fresh lemon juice
    Kosher salt
  1 tsp. shallots
  1 tsp. clarified butter or
    margarine
  2 oz. Triple Sec
    Juice of 1 lime
12 slices of pear
  2 Tbsps. honey
  1 cup demi-glace
½ cup heavy cream
  8 slices of avocado

To prepare the duck, poke 4 holes under the ducks' legs to help defat them while cooking. Coat thoroughly with fresh lemon juice and then sprinkle kosher salt over entire duck. Place ducks, breast side up, on roasting racks. Cook for 40 minutes or until lightly browned.

Reduce heat to 300° and turn ducks over. Drain the fat out of the pan. Cook 20 minutes and drain fat again. Turn ducks over one final time and cook 20 minutes more. Remove from oven and let cool. Once ducks are cool enough to handle, split them in half and remove backbone and breastbone from each half.

Just before assembling with sauce for serving, place duck halves on a cookie sheet, skin side up, with a little water in the pan to keep ducks from sticking. Place pan on bottom rack of oven with the broiler on high and cook until skin is crispy, approximately 5 to 7 minutes.

For the pear and avocado sauce, sauté the shallots in butter. Add Triple Sec and reduce. Add the remaining ingredients one at a time and continue to cook until desired consistency. Remove from heat.

To serve, place sauce directly on serving plate. Place ducks from broiler on top of sauce. Garnish top of ducks with alternate slices of pear and avocado in a fan-shaped design.

Coconut Rum Caramel Custard with Roasted Banana Sauce

Stir 2 cups of granulated sugar, ¾ cup water and cream of tartar over low heat until sugar is dissolved. Let cook until the mixture turns light brown in color. Pour the caramel mixture into a two-quart soufflé dish or into individual cups and swirl around to coat the sides.

Mix the whole eggs, egg yolks, and 1 cup sugar together gently in a bowl so that no bubbles form.

Bring 4 cups cream and the toasted coconut to a boil, remove from heat and slowly add to the egg mixture. Add the rum to the cream and egg mixture and pour through a fine sieve into molds.

Place the custard into a bain-marie and bake approximately 1½ hours or until done.

Roast the bananas at 450° until skin becomes dark brown and begins to ooze. Cool, peel and set aside.

Combine 1 cup sugar and ¾ cup water and caramelize over low heat. Add 1½ cup cream to the caramel and stir to cool down. Add the bananas and mix thoroughly. Strain through a fine sieve.

To serve, run a knife around the edge of the mold, invert the mold on a serving dish, and drizzle with custard banana sauce.

Trade Secret: Garnish with toasted coconut and several slices of banana for a truly decadent appearance.

Serves 8
Preparation Time:
  1 Hour
Cooking Time:
  1 Hour, 30 Minutes
Pre-heat oven to 350°

  4 cups sugar
1½ cups water
  ½ tsp. cream of tartar
  4 whole eggs
  8 egg yolks
5½ cups cream
  ¼ lb. toasted coconut
  ½ cup rum
  3 large bananas

★

DAN'L WEBSTER INN

CONTEMPORARY AMERICAN CUISINE
149 Main Street
Sandwich, Massachusetts
(508) 888-3623
Lunch 11:45PM–4:00PM
Dinner 4:30PM–6:00PM
AVERAGE DINNER FOR TWO: $35

T he gracious hospitality and heritage of this proud inn is conveyed in the Colonial New England decor and costumed servers. The original tavern, built in 1692, was destroyed by fire in 1971 and rebuilt in a fashion to satisfy modern tastes, yet generate the charm and warmth of the original structure.

The expansion included a gracious sunlit conservatory and a wine cellar equal to the finest in New England. The menu developed into classical American cuisine that has been awarded national recognition each year.

Regional dishes from chef/owner Robert Catania such as Fresh Swordfish topped with a Sun-dried Tomato Butter and native Cape Scallops Sautéed with Hand-filled Cheese Tortellini, then finished with fresh Pesto share the menu with homemade soups, fresh salads, sandwiches and whole grain pizza.

DAN'L WEBSTER INN'S MENU FOR FOUR

Smoked Duckling Salad

Macadamia and Cashew Crusted Striped Bass

Pineapple Mascarpone Velvet

Grilled Duckling Salad

Brush olive oil onto the duck breasts and season with salt and pepper. Grill until medium rare in center, about 8 minutes. Cool, then slice the breast thin at a 45° angle.

Place lettuce on 4 individual plates. Arrange duck slices on bed of lettuce and top with your favorite vinaigrette. Sprinkle tops of salads with chopped pecans.

Trade Secret: A garnish of edible flowers is a beautiful accompaniment to this salad.

Serves 4
Preparation Time:
  30 Minutes

  2 **duck breasts, ½ lb. each**
  2 **Tbsps. olive oil**
    Salt and pepper to taste
  1 **head bib lettuce**
  ¼ **cup pecan pieces**

Macadamia and Cashew Crusted Striped Bass

Serves 4
Preparation Time:
 1 Hour

- ⅓ cup unsalted macadamia nuts
- ⅓ cup unsalted cashews
- ¾ cup fresh unseasoned bread crumbs
- ¾ tsp. salt
  Pinch of cayenne pepper
- 4 striped bass filets, 6 oz. each
- ½ cup flour
- 3 eggs, beaten
- 8 Tbsps. (1 stick) unsalted butter
- 2 Tbsps. vegetable oil
- 2 ripe mangos
- ⅓ cup Riesling wine
- 1 Tbsp. fresh lemon juice
- ½ tsp. garlic, chopped
- 2 Tbsps. honey

In a food processor, finely chop nuts, bread crumbs, salt and pepper. Dredge boneless, skinless filets in flour. Shake off excess flour, then dip into egg wash and bread crumb mixture.

In a large sauté pan, sauté filets in 2 Tbsps. butter and vegetable oil. Cook until brown on each side.

Purée mangos and set aside. In a small saucepan, reduce wine with lemon juice and garlic until almost fully reduced. Add mango purée and honey. Season to taste with salt and pepper. Remove from heat and whip in butter.

Serve filets drizzled with the warm mango sauce.

Pineapple Mascarpone Velvet

I n a medium-sized saucepan, melt the butter with lemon juice and brown sugar. Add split vanilla bean and ginger. Cook for 3 minutes while stirring over medium heat. Add the pineapple chunks and rum. Cook over medium-high heat while stirring for 8 minutes or until pineapple begins to soften.

Remove pineapple with slotted spoon and reserve, leaving liquid in pan over medium-high heat. Allow to reduce until a syrup texture is achieved.

Cool both pineapple and syrup, then combine and reserve.

Place mascarpone, cream, honey and lemon juice in an electric mixer and whip until a fluffy yet firm texture is achieved. Do not over-whip or it will separate.

In 8 tulip glasses, place 2 Tbsps. of pineapple mixture on the bottom. Top with 2 inches of mascarpone mixture, then top again with 2 tablespoons of pineapple mixture.

Garnish with a dollop of whipped cream and a mint leaf.

Serves 8
Preparation Time:
3 Hours

- 1 Tbsp. unsalted butter
- 1 tsp. fresh lemon juice
- ¾ cup packed light brown sugar
- 1 whole vanilla bean, split
- 1½ Tbsps. fresh ginger root, chopped
- ½ pineapple, cut into chunks
- ¼ cup dark rum
- 1 cup mascarpone cheese
- 1 cup heavy cream
- 2 Tbsps. honey
- 1 tsp. fresh lemon juice
  Whipped cream garnish
  Mint leaves, garnish

★

LAMBERT'S COVE COUNTRY INN AND RESTAURANT

NEW ENGLAND CUISINE
Lambert's Cove Road
West Tisbury, Massachusetts
(508) 693-2298
Dinner 6PM–9PM
Sunday brunch 11AM–1:30PM
AVERAGE DINNER FOR TWO: $56

T he Lambert's Cove Country Inn and Restaurant dates back to 1790. Located in a quiet and secluded setting, this elegant country inn is surrounded by seven acres of lawns, gardens and vine-covered stone walls, apple orchards and towering pine trees.

The dining room is cozy and romantic, featuring hardwood floors, fireplace, soft lighting and music. The hearty New England cuisine features island seafood, in-season vegetables just-picked from nearby gardens, veal, beef, homemade soups, breads and delicious desserts.

Menu highlights include Duck Galantine with Pistachios and Olives, Grilled Swordfish Steak with a Brown Butter of Chunk Lobster, Macadamia Nuts and fresh Sorrel, and Roast Boneless Lamb Loin with a Mango Chutney.

The Sunday brunch menu features Strawberry Mascarpone-filled Crepes, Poached Salmon Filets with Hollandaise Sauce and Herb Roasted Potatoes or Cinnamon French Toast with warm Maple Syrup.

LAMBERT'S COVE COUNTRY INN'S MENU FOR FOUR

Shrimp, Scallops and Andouille Sausage Stew

Grilled Swordfish with Mangos and Sweet Peppers

Vanilla Mousse with Fresh Raspberries and Blackberries

Shrimp, Scallops and Andouille Sausage Stew

I n a 5-gallon stock pot, heat the olive oil and sauté the onions, celery, garlic and both bell peppers. When the celery and onions are translucent, add the Andouille sausage.

When the sausage is browned, add the quartered tomatoes and fresh basil. Let simmer for 5 minutes to start softening the tomatoes. Add the wine, saffron and spices and simmer for 15 minutes.

Add the rice, shrimp, scallops and 3 cups water. Make sure to add any juice from shrimp and scallops, since this adds a wonderful flavor. Simmer for 1 hour. Rice will absorb the excess liquid.

Trade Secret: This is excellent served with French bread or corn muffins.

Serves 4
Preparation Time:
  1 Hour, 30 Minutes

  3 Tbsps. olive oil
  1 onion, minced
  2 celery stalks, diced
  2 cloves garlic
  1 green bell pepper, diced
  1 red bell pepper, diced
  ½ lb. Andouille sausage
  6 tomatoes, quartered
  3 Tbsps. fresh basil
  2 cups white wine
  6 threads saffron
  ½ tsp. ground coriander
  ½ tsp. ground cumin
  1 cup rice
  ¼ lb. shrimp
  ¼ lb. scallops
  3 cups water

Grilled Swordfish with Mangos and Sweet Pepper Relish

Serves 4
Preparation Time:
  30 Minutes

  1 Tbsp. vegetable oil
  2 tsps. fresh ginger,
    minced
  1 tsp. fresh garlic,
    minced
  2 Tbsps. Bermuda onion,
    minced
  1 red bell pepper, diced
  1 ripe mango, diced
    Pinch of curry powder
  2 cups dry white wine
    Salt and pepper to
    taste
  4 swordfish steaks, ½ lb.
    each, 1" thick

I n a small saucepan, heat the oil. Add the ginger, garlic and onion. Sauté until the onion is translucent. Add the bell pepper, mango, curry and white wine, and simmer for 10 minutes. Add salt and pepper to taste. Set aside.

Grill the swordfish steaks over high heat, about 3 to 4 minutes per side. The steaks should be seared on the outside and just cooked through, yet moist on the inside.

Serve immediately with the warm mango and sweet pepper relish.

★

Vanilla Mousse with Fresh Raspberries and Blackberries

Combine the heavy cream, vanilla and ⅓ cup of the sugar in a mixing bowl. Whip until extra stiff. Do not over-whip or this mixture will not fold together with other ingredients. Place in a separate container and refrigerate.

In a small saucepan, combine ⅓ cup sugar with water over medium heat. Using a candy thermometer to determine when the syrup reaches 225°, begin whipping the egg whites together in a food processor or mixer at high speed. The egg whites will become stiff, with high points. (Do not turn off the mixer or the egg whites will fall.) When the syrup reaches 238°, turn the mixer to medium speed and slowly add the hot syrup. Mix the egg whites with syrup in mixer for 15 minutes on a low speed to cook the eggs.

After 15 minutes of mixing, fold the egg whites into the whipped cream. Fold both berries into the mousse mixture. Pour the mousse into individual ramekins and refrigerate for 1 hour.

Trade Secrets: In this recipe, timing is very important. It is recommended that all measurements be made before starting the recipe.

Fresh raspberry purée is a nice accompaniment to this dessert.

Serves 4
Preparation Time:
  45 Minutes
(note refrigeration time)

⅓ cup heavy cream
1 tsp. vanilla extract
⅔ cup sugar
2 Tbsps. water
3 egg whites, room temperature
½ pt. fresh raspberries
½ pt. fresh blackberries

☆

L'ÉTOILE

CONTEMPORARY FRENCH CUISINE
At the Charlotte Inn
South Summer Street
Edgartown, Massachusetts
(508) 627-5187
Dinner 6:30PM–9:30PM
AVERAGE DINNER FOR TWO: Prix Fixe $48 per person

Located on the first floor of the historic Charlotte Inn, L'Étoile is a contemporary French restaurant serving some of the best French cuisine on the island. The owners of the inn, Paula and Gery Conover, have leased the restaurant for the last 2½ years to Chef Michael Brisson and his wife, Joan Parzanese.

The restaurant looks like an enclosed sunporch and the Conovers have decorated the 17-table dining room in crisp white linens, bright greenery and paintings of fruits and vegetables. The elegant restaurant is cozy and romantic at dinner, and bright and inviting at breakfast. The dining room also overlooks a 20-seat patio where guests can delight in an outdoor meal on a warm summer's night.

Guests feast on mouth-watering meals with fresh local fruits and greens, and the bounty of the Atlantic. Menu highlights include native Lobster and Scallops with a Vegetable Taliatelle, and Roasted Lamb Noisettes with Warm Goat Cheese and Roasted Eggplant Millefeuille. Appetizers are just as inviting with items like Sautéed Ravioli of Rock Shrimp and Salmon Mousselines, and Ossetra Caviar with Mascarpone and Scallion-filled Crêpes. Fresh raspberries bought from local Thimble Farm go into the White Chocolate and Raspberry Puff Pastry Tart, and L'Étoile's own Rhubarb Tart is a delicious creation.

L'ETOILE'S MENU FOR FOUR

Oyster and Spinach Custard with Saffron Beurre Blanc

Foie Gras with Mango and Raspberries

White Chocolate and Raspberry Puff Pastry Tart

Oyster and Spinach Custard with Saffron Beurre Blanc

Shuck the oysters, rinse and pat dry with towel. Steam the spinach and rinse it in cold water. Squeeze the liquid out and chop lightly.

Place the eggs and yolks in a blender and purée. Add 1¼ cups cream and spinach and pulse. Season with salt and white pepper. Combine 1 Tbsp. cornstarch and 1½ Tbsps. water, add to egg mixture and pulse.

Butter 4 molds (½ cup muffin tins or egg molds). Skim any foam off the top of the custard mixture. Fill the molds half way. Dredge the oysters in cornstarch, shaking off any excess. Place two oysters in each mold. Fill the molds just shy of the top.

Place the mold in a bain-marie with water ¾ up the side of the mold. Cook for 18 minutes or until the custard is firm. Remove from oven and let cool 5 minutes. Prepare the beurre blanc sauce by heating 3 Tbsps. white wine with the saffron. Reserve and set aside.

In a saucepan, over low heat, reduce the vinegar, wine and shallots until there is barely any liquid left. Add 1 Tbsp. heavy cream, then whisk in the cold butter 1 Tbsp. at a time.

Remove from heat. Strain, season with salt and pepper and some of the saffron liquid to taste. Stir in the diced tomato just before serving.

With a small rubber spatula, free custards from the molds and drizzle with the sauce.

Serves 4
Preparation Time:
  35 Minutes
Pre-heat oven to 325°

- 8 fresh oysters
- 1½ cups spinach, cleaned
- 2 extra large eggs
- 2 egg yolks
- 1¼ cups + 1 Tbsp. heavy cream
  Salt and pepper
- ½ cup + 1 Tbsp. cornstarch
- 1½ Tbsps. water
- ½ cup + 3 Tbsps. white wine
- 6 strands of saffron
- 3 Tbsps. champagne vinegar
- 2 Tbsps. shallots, chopped
- 8 Tbsps. (1 stick) cold butter, sliced
- 2 plum tomatoes, peeled, cored, diced

Foie Gras with Mango and Raspberries

Serves 4
Preparation Time:
20 Minutes
(note refrigeration time)

¾ lb. goose or duck liver
2 Tbsps. cracked sea salt
2 Tbsps. cracked white
   pepper
½ tsp. nutmeg
½ tsp. allspice
1½ Tbsps. shallots,
   chopped
1¾ cups leeks, julienne
3 Tbsps. champagne
   vinegar
⅓ cup Muscat wine
½ cup chicken stock
1 bay leaf
⅓ cup mango purée
1 Tbsp. heavy cream
3 Tbsps. cold butter
   Flour
½ pt. raspberries
1 mango, sliced
2 Tbsps. chopped chives

Prepare the foie gras at room temperature. Separate the side lobe and remove the exposed veins and nerves by pulling gently with a towel. Lay the liver flat and cut it into ⅜" slices. Season each slice with cracked sea salt, white pepper, nutmeg and allspice. Press the seasonings into the slices and chill.

For the sauce, use a small saucepan to sweat the shallots and ¼ cup leeks in the champagne vinegar until soft. Add the Muscat wine and chicken stock, bay leaf and reduce by half. Strain, pressing the solids firmly against the strainer and discard.

Return the liquid to the saucepan and bring to a simmer. Whisk in the mango purée. Reduce to a ½ cup. Stir in the cream and simmer, then whisk in the butter and season with salt and pepper. Add 1½ cups leek julienne just to wilt it. Remove and reserve for garnish.

Heat a large sauté pan over medium-high heat. Coat the liver slices lightly with flour and place them into the pan. No fat is needed. Sauté each side 30 seconds for medium-rare. Place on a towel to drain any excess fat.

Arrange 5 raspberries in a star shape around the plate and wrap mango slices around the raspberries, to look like a flower. Ladle the sauce equally on the plates and place the foie gras in the middle of the plate. Arrange the wilted leek julienne over the top of the liver. Sprinkle with chives.

White Chocolate and Raspberry Puff Pastry Tart

For the tart shell, roll the puff pastry very thin to fit into the rectangular tart pan. Chill for 15 minutes and then with a fork, prick the dough so the rising is controlled.

Bake the tart shell until it starts to brown, about 18 minutes, then egg wash the shell and return to the oven for 5 minutes more until it is golden brown. Let cool for 10 minutes and then brush on the melted dark chocolate. This seals the tart shell from any moisture from the filling. Let cool at room temperature while making filling.

In a double boiler, melt the white chocolate, butter, ¼ cup cream, and vanilla. Stir until mixture is melted and tepid.

Whip ¾ cup cream until soft peaks form and gently fold it into the white chocolate mixture until smooth. Do not overfold. Pour filling into the pastry shell and dot with raspberries. Chill for 45 minutes.

Shave the white chocolate, at room temperature, with a vegetable peeler into a flat container to yield 3 cups. Chill 5 minutes in freezer.

When the filling has firmed, place the curls standing up on the tart. Cover the whole surface and chill until ready to serve.

Serves 4
Preparation Time:
 1 Hour, 30 Minutes
Pre-heat oven to 350°

 4"×12" tart pan with
  removable bottom
1 sheet of puff pastry,
  6 oz.
3 oz. dark chocolate,
  melted
1 egg beaten with
  1 Tbsp. water for egg
  wash
6 oz. white chocolate,
  chopped
2 Tbsps. butter
1 cup heavy cream
2 tsps. vanilla extract
¾ cup heavy cream
  whipped to soft peaks
  White chocolate
  shavings, garnish,
  about 5 oz.

WARRINERS RESTAURANT

AMERICAN CUISINE
Box 407
Post Office Square
Edgartown, Massachusetts
(508) 627-4488
Dinner 6PM–9PM
AVERAGE DINNER FOR TWO: $75

Owner Sam Warriner runs two restaurants under one roof. Warriners is a luxurious, reservations-only dining room in the library. Adjoining is the bistro-style Sam's, with a casual elegance where guests can wait at the bar to be seated and enjoy a less formal, no frills menu.

The cuisine in Warriners is regional American while the setting is English. The mahogany tables in the library are adorned with fine Dudson china (including matching vases and salt and pepper shakers), flower vases, and small brass lamps. Soft lighting, Queen Anne chairs, fireplaces and a bookcase filled to the brim complete the home-like ambiance.

Honored with the 1989 award of excellence by Wine Spectator magazine, Warriners offers an excellent and extensive wine list. Impressively, there are about 150 wines to choose from — ranging in price from affordable to extravagant.

The menu is an ever-changing creative assortment of foods. Fresh fish of the day is announced and priced daily while other entrées like the seared Center Cut of Sirloin with Four Peppercorns and Thyme with Bass Ale Sauce can be found on the menu at any given time. The sautéed Cape Pogue Bay Scallops with a Melange of Radicchio, Endive and Spinach, or the Linguine and Lobster with Green Onions, Whiskey and Shallot Cream Sauce are two other possibilities. The desserts change daily as well and can include a decadent White Chocolate Mousse with Raspberries.

WARRINER'S MENU FOR EIGHT

Salmon Gravlax with

Tarragon Mustard Horseradish Sauce

Sautéed Scallops with Endive, Radicchio and Spinach

Salmon Gravlax

R inse salmon filet in cold water and pat dry with paper towel. Trim sides and ends if necessary so you have a nice rectangular piece.

Mix salt and sugar in a small bowl. Place filet on a large piece of plastic film, coat both sides of filet with sugar/salt mixture and wrap tightly with plastic film then wrap with foil. Place the salmon between two cookie sheets with at least 10 lbs. of weight on top and refrigerate for 24 hours.

Remove salmon from wrapping and rinse in cold water, pat dry and place on a piece of plastic wrap. Mix all the chopped herbs and divide into equal parts. Do the same with the zest and divide the cognac and black pepper in half. Then sprinkle half the ingredients over one side of the salmon in this order: cognac, black pepper, zest and herbs. Flip filet over on plastic wrap and repeat. Wrap lightly with plastic wrap, then foil, place between cookie sheets, press and refrigerate for another 24 hours.

Top salmon with the Tarragon Mustard Horseradish Sauce, on the following page.

Serves 8
Preparation Time:
  1 Hour, 30 Minutes
(note marinating time)

  1 lb. salmon filet with skin & pin bones removed
  2 Tbsps. Kosher salt
  1 Tbsp. brown sugar
  ¼ cup fresh parsley, chopped
  1½ Tbsps. fresh oregano, chopped
  1½ Tbsps. fresh sage, chopped
  1 Tbsp. fresh thyme, chopped
     Zest of ½ an orange
     Zest of ½ a lemon
     Zest of ½ a lime
  1 Tbsp. cognac
  ½ tsp. fresh black pepper, coarsely ground

☆

Tarragon Mustard Horseradish Sauce

Yield: 1 Cup
Preparation Time:
  15 Minutes

  2 **large egg yolks at room**
    temperature
  1 **Tbsp. warm water**
  1 **cup peanut oil**
  1 **Tbsp. tarragon,**
    chopped
 ½ **tsp. honey**
  2 **tsps. fresh lemon juice**
1½ **tsps. coarse-grained**
    mustard
1½ **tsps. prepared**
    horseradish
  3 **Tbsps. white wine**
 ½ **cup red onion, minced**
 ½ **cup capers, rinsed,**
    drained

Place the yolks and warm water in a food processor. Mix for 1 minute, then drizzle oil to make mayonnaise. If the mayonnaise becomes very thick, before adding oil, add the liquid ingredients.

Add the tarragon, honey, lemon juice, mustard and horseradish and mix well. Adjust consistency with white wine. Sauce should flow, but not be runny.

To serve over the salmon gravlax, slice the salmon thinly on a bias and arrange on a plate with minced red onion and capers, then dot plate with the sauce.

★

Sautéed Scallops
with Radicchio, Endive and Spinach

T o make the vinaigrette, combine the first five ingredients in a bowl, mix well and adjust any ingredient according to individual taste. Just keep in mind that the endive and radicchio are on the bitter side.

Remove the stems from the spinach, wash and let dry thoroughly. Cut the spinach into thin strips. Cut the radicchio in half, remove the core and julienne into thin strips. Do the same with the endive and mix all three in a bowl.

Rinse the scallops in water and remove the tough elastic muscle that attaches the scallops to the shell, and let them drain thoroughly.

Heat two very large sauté pans on the stove. Divide the butter and peanut oil between the two pans and let it reach the smoking point.

Carefully place the scallops in the pans, shake the pans vigorously and cook for about 1 minute. Do not overcook.

Add the julienne vegetables and sauté briefly. Now, with pans still on the heat, add the vinaigrette, salt and pepper and mix well. Remove from pans immediately and serve.

Serves 8
Preparation Time:
  1 Hour

⅓ cup balsamic vinegar
1 cup extra virgin olive oil
1 Tbsp. brown sugar
1 tsp. whole grain mustard
    Kosher salt & freshly ground white pepper to taste
2 bunches spinach
1 large head raddichio
2 heads Belgian endive
3 lbs. bay scallops
¾ cup clarified butter
¼ cup peanut oil

☆

THE WOODBOX

CALIFORNIA-FRENCH CONTINENTAL CUISINE
29 Fair Street
Nantucket, Massachusetts
(508) 228-0587
Breakfast daily 8:30AM–11AM
Dinner nightly 6:45PM seating and 9PM seating
AVERAGE DINNER FOR TWO: $70

The three intimate dining rooms on the first floor of this sea captain's house reflect their charming 1709 rustic origins. The decor is characterized by wide plank floors, exposed wooden beams, huge fireplaces, and Colonial-style furniture. Tables are appointed with delicate English china, fresh flowers and candles.

Chef Joseph Keller describes his style of cooking as influenced by the French and tempered by California and Southwestern cuisines. Dinner begins with a basketful of rich piping hot popovers, for which The Woodbox is noted. A classic appetizer that follows may be Crabtina, a delicate mixture of king crab meat tossed with a bleu cheese and horseradish dressing or a Goat Cheese and Pesto Tart. Entrees such as Rack of Lamb Provencale, delicately flavored with herbed garlic bread crumbs and Cremini mushroom caps finished in a Beaujolais sauce, or a crisp Roast Duck served in a lightly sweet glaze made from three-berry casis. Among the dessert selections there is one specialty of the house you will find nowhere else on Nantucket: Bananas Foster. It's a delightful combination of honey and banana liqueur drizzled over fresh bananas and vanilla ice cream.

The Woodbox is a restaurant run by people who really love to cook for people who love to eat.

THE WOODBOX'S MENU FOR FOUR

Smoked Salmon Quesadilla

Medallions of Venison

Chocolate Bourbon Pecan Cake

Smoked Salmon Quesadilla

Prepare the horseradish cream in a large mixing bowl by blending together the goat cheese, horseradish, sour cream and 1 tsp. dill. Salt and pepper to taste. Set aside.

Sauté the flour tortillas for 1 minute on each side to brown lightly. Spread the horseradish cream evenly over each tortilla. Arrange the smoked salmon over cream and sprinkle with the remaining dill.

Slice and serve immediately.

Serves 4
Preparation Time:
   10 Minutes

- 2 oz. mild goat cheese
- 1 Tbsp. fresh horseradish, grated *used 1 lg tsp. prepared*
- 1 Tbsp. sour cream
- 3 tsps. dill, chopped — *used dried*
  Salt and pepper to taste
- 2 flour tortillas
- 4 thin slices smoked salmon

*** Very good
Put tortilla in oven to crispa little rather than sauteing*

*9/6/93
El has decided he no longer cares for this*

Medallions of Venison

Serves 4
Preparation Time:
  45 Minutes

  8 **medallions of deer
     tenderloin, 3 oz. each**
     **Salt and pepper to
     taste**
     Flour for dredging
 ⅓ **cup olive oil**
 ½ **lb. morels or other
     wild mushrooms**
  6 **thyme sprigs or 1 tsp.
     dry thyme**
 ½ **cup port wine**
  1 **Tbsp. lingonberries,
     drained**
1½ **cups heavy cream**
  1 **cup beef stock**
  1 **carrot, peeled, sliced
     into thin strips**
 20 **snow peas**
 ¼ **cup dry white wine**
     **Thyme sprigs as
     garnish**

Trim the tenderloins of any fat and silver skin. Cut into ¾" slices. Press the medallions flat with your hand on the bottom of a flat pan. Season with salt and pepper and dredge with flour, shaking off any excess.

In a sauté pan over medium-high heat, add ¼ cup of the olive oil and the medallions. Sauté for 3 to 4 minutes per side or until medium rare.

After the medallions have cooked, add the wild mushrooms and sauté quickly. Remove the meat from the pan, leaving only the mushrooms, and add the thyme and pepper.

Flame the mushrooms with the port, putting out the flames with a pot cover. Add the lingonberries, cream, and beef stock to the pan. Reduce over high heat until sauce is reduced by half.

While the sauce is reducing, heat the remaining oil in a small sauté pan until hot. Add the carrots and snow peas. Sauté, stirring frequently for 3 minutes. Add the wine and reduce until it has almost evaporated. Season with salt and pepper, then set aside.

To serve, place 2 medallions on each plate and drizzle with sauce. Arrange the vegetables on either side and garnish with sprigs of thyme.

☆

Chocolate Bourbon Pecan Cake

O il or butter the bottom and sides of a 12" springform pan. Place parchment paper on bottom of pan and dust bottom and sides with sugar. Set aside.

Melt ¾ lb. (1½ cups) chocolate in a double boiler. Cut the butter into small pieces and stir into the chocolate until melted. Set aside and keep warm.

Separate eggs. Whip the egg whites until foamy. Add half the sugar and continue whipping until the egg whites are stiff. Set aside.

Whip the remaining sugar and egg yolks until ribbony. Mix in the melted chocolate and bourbon. Alternately fold in the ground pecans and egg whites. Pour the batter into the prepared springform pan. Bake at 300° for 1½ to 1¾ hours. Remove from the oven and cool.

Prepare the glaze by melting ¾ lb. (1½ cups) chocolate in a double boiler, stir in vegetable oil. Remove from heat to cool.

Remove the cake from the springform pan and place inverted on icing rack. Ladle glaze over cake and spread to cover top and sides. Garnish by placing pecan halves around the top rim. Refrigerate cake for 30 minutes to allow glaze to harden before serving.

Preparation Time:
   2 Hours
Cooling Time:
   30 Minutes

1½ lbs. semi-sweet
   chocolate, chopped
2 sticks unsalted butter
8 eggs
1½ cups sugar
½ cup bourbon
1 lb. pecans, finely
   ground
⅓ cup vegetable oil
18 large pecan halves

BLANTYRE

P.O. Box 995
Lenox, Massachusetts 01240
(413) 637-3556 May–November
(413) 298-3806 Winter
ROOM RATES: $220–$575
AMENITIES: Twenty-three bedrooms and suites, many with fireplaces, all with private bath, restaurant, lounge, room service, 85-acre grounds, outdoor pool, jacuzzi, sauna, tennis courts, croquet lawns. Breakfast included. Near Tanglewood Music Festival, the Norman Rockwell Museum and many antique galleries.
DIRECTIONS: 120 miles west of Boston. Take I-90 East to Exit 2. Take Route 20 West for 3 miles.

Blantyre is a Tudor-style mansion built in 1902. Its grandeur and European style make it unique on American soil. Built to replicate a Scottish manor, Blantyre's gothic woodwork and decor are fit for the most discriminating nobility and are complemented by world-class service. Hand-carved antiques grace the spacious rooms and suites throughout the Main House, the carriage house and the cottages. The inn was the first in America to win the coveted International Welcome Award from Relais et Chateaux, and Zagat rated it in the top ten resorts and inns nationwide, number one in New England.

The 85-acre grounds are available for walks, as well as tennis courts, croquet lawns, and an outdoor pool for guest recreation. Afterwards, enjoy the sauna or jacuzzi. In the evening, a lavishly prepared five-course French meal is available in the restaurant. Chef David Lawson prepares such fare as Saddle of Venison Roasted in a Salt Crust, and Pumpkin Gnocchi with native Wild Blueberries.

Crab Cakes with Red and Yellow Pepper Sauce and Crispy Fried Leeks

Beat 2 eggs slightly and combine with remaining ingredients. Shape into 3" patties, ½" thick.

Coat in flour, then beaten egg, then bread crumbs.

Fry in vegetable oil over medium-high heat, adding a little butter to the pan when cakes have set. Turn carefully, browning both sides.

Transfer to a sheet pan and finish in the oven at 375° until cakes puff a little, about 8 minutes.

To serve, spoon some of the yellow pepper sauce onto half of each serving plate. Cover the other half of each plate with red pepper sauce. With the tip of a paring knife or toothpick, draw swirls through the two sauces. Heap a little mound of the fried leek julienne in the center of each plate and place a crab cake on top of the leeks.

Serves 4
Preparation Time:
  15 Minutes
Cooking Time:
  20 Minutes

  2 eggs
  1 lb. crab meat
  ½ cup onion, finely
    chopped
  1 cup fine bread crumbs
  ¼ tsp. dry mustard
  2 Tbsps. parsley,
    chopped
  1 Tbsp. mayonnaise
  1 Tbsp. Worcestershire
    sauce
  ½ tsp. white pepper
  1 tsp. salt
    Flour, beaten egg, and
    bread crumbs for
    coating
    Oil and butter for
    frying

  Red and Yellow
  Pepper Sauce, recipe
  follows on page 166.

  Fried Leek Julienne,
  recipe follows on
  page 167.

★

Red and Yellow Pepper Sauces

Serves 4
Preparation Time:
  20 Minutes

  1 **red bell pepper**
  1 **yellow bell pepper**
  1 **cup vegetable oil**
  2 **egg yolks**
     Juice of ½ lemon
  1 **garlic clove, finely**
     minced
     Salt and white pepper
     to taste
  ⅛ **tsp. cayenne pepper**

ub the peppers lightly with vegetable oil, then char the skins over the flame of a gas stove or under a broiler until blistered.

Put peppers in a bowl and cover tightly for 10 minutes to loosen the skin.

Make a stiff mayonnaise with the egg yolks, lemon juice and remaining vegetable oil. Season with garlic, salt, pepper and cayenne. Divide the mayonnaise into two small bowls.

Peel the peppers, cut them in half and discard the seeds and stems.

In a food processor, purée the yellow pepper and whisk into one bowl of mayonnaise. Repeat with the red pepper. Adjust seasoning. The sauces should be pourable: whisk in a few drops warm water if necessary to achieve the right consistency.

Cover each bowl and reserve in a cool place until ready.

Fried Leek Julienne

Prepare a fine julienne of leeks using the white and tender yellow-green portions. Rinse and drain well. Reserve on a paper towel.

Heat oil until one strand of leek sizzles vigorously when tested. Fry the leeks in small batches. When they become slightly golden, remove from oil with a slotted spoon and reserve on a paper towel.

Repeat until all leeks are fried. Store in a warm place until ready to serve. These may be made up to two hours ahead.

Serves 4
Preparation Time:
   15 Minutes

1 medium leek, about
   1½″ diameter
   Vegetable oil for frying

CHARLOTTE INN

South Summer Street
Edgartown, Massachusetts 02539
(508) 627-4751
ROOM RATES: $125–$350
AMENITIES: Twenty-four comfortable, antique-furnished rooms. Many with working fireplaces. Full-service restaurant, L'Etoile, as well as an art gallery and gift shop.
DIRECTIONS: From Vineyard Haven, take Beach Road to Main Street in Edgartown. Follow Main Street to South Summer Street and turn right on South Summer to the inn.

Nestled in a cozy garden surrounded by brick paths, flowerbeds, lawns and latticework, the Charlotte Inn has watched over Edgartown's shady South Summer Street for over 130 years. Built in 1860, the inn was once a sea captain's home.

Plush carpets and lofty ceilings are invitations to linger a while. Warm, deep-hued wallpapers and vases of freshly cut flowers add to the intimacy. Fine English antiques, as well as original paintings and engravings grace the walls. This sort of meticulous attention to detail is one of the inn's trademarks...no two rooms are alike.

Complimentary breakfast is served in the open-air terrace or the bow-windowed conservatory dining room.

Morning Glory Muffins

I n a large mixing bowl, combine the flour, sugar, baking soda, cinnamon and salt.

In a separate bowl, beat the eggs and slowly whisk in the oil. Stir in the carrots, apple, raisins, coconut, pecans and vanilla. Slowly add this to the flour mixture.

Pour batter into 18 greased muffin tins. Bake at 325° for 20 to 25 minutes.

Yields: 18 muffins
Preparation Time:
30 minutes

2 cups flour
1 cup sugar
2 tsps. baking soda
2 tsps. cinnamon
½ tsp. salt
3 eggs, slightly beaten
1 cup vegetable oil
2 cups grated carrots,
    about 3 carrots
1 apple, peeled, grated
½ cup raisins
½ cup shredded coconut
½ cup pecans, chopped
2 tsps. vanilla extract

☆

LAMBERT'S COVE COUNTRY INN

Lambert's Cove Road
West Tisbury, Martha's Vineyard, Massachusetts 02575
(508) 693-2298
ROOM RATES: $95–$125
AMENITIES: Fifteen rooms with private baths, tennis courts, 4-star restaurant.
DIRECTIONS: From Vineyard Haven harbor take State Road to Lambert's Cove Road. Turn right on Lambert's Cove Road and follow signs to the inn.

The Lambert's Cove Inn provides quiet and seclusion amid a country setting of tall pines, 150-year-old vine-covered stone walls, spacious lawns, rambling gardens and an apple orchard.

This is an inn for those who seek a place where both mind and body can be restored, far from the noise and crowds of town and city. The pace is leisurely, the mood relaxed and the style informal.

The original part of the main inn was built in 1790, as a farmhouse, and some of the hand-hewn rafters from that period may be seen in the upstairs bedrooms. In the 1920's the farmhouse was enlarged to serve as the estate residence of a former owner, an amateur horti-culturist, world traveler and literary figure of note. It is in this dwelling that half of the guest rooms are located. The remainder are in a converted barn and a carriage house, renovated for guest use.

Each room has distinctive charm. Many open onto individual decks. One has its own greenhouse sitting room, a cherished horticultural legacy from the past. Many guests relax after dinner with dessert and coffee in the beautiful library just across from the dining room, which also features a fireplace.

Strawberry Mascarpone Filled Crêpes

Prepare the filling by puréeing the strawberries in a food processor or blender. Bring strawberries, 1 cup sugar and water to a boil over medium heat. Boil for 8 to 10 minutes, stirring constantly. Remove from heat and allow mixture to cool and thicken.

In a mixing bowl, combine the mascarpone and 1½ cups powdered sugar. Add ½ cup of the cooled strawberry sauce. Set aside.

In a double boiler on low heat, melt the chocolate. When melted, stir in ¾ cup cream until well incorporated. Set aside.

Beat 2 cups cream with ½ cup powdered sugar and 1 tsp. vanilla until stiff. Set aside.

In a food processor or blender, add the eggs, milk, butter, cornstarch, 1 Tbsp. sugar, salt and 1 tsp. vanilla. Blend on high for 20 seconds or until batter is mixed.

In a crêpe pan hot enough for a drop of batter to sizzle, pour in 4 Tbsps. of the batter over medium-high heat. Swirl the batter around the pan slowly and evenly. When the bottom of the crêpe is just starting to color, flip it over. Cook just a second more in the pan and slide the crêpe out onto parchment paper. Return the pan to the heat and repeat the procedure, to make 12 crêpes.

To assemble, fill each crêpe with 2 Tbsps. of the mascarpone mixture and strawberry sauce. Roll up crêpes and place seam side down on a serving plate. Spoon chocolate sauce over each crêpe and garnish with whipped cream, chocolate shavings and sliced strawberries.

Serves 6
Preparation Time:
  45 Minutes

  1 pt. strawberries
  1 cup + 1 Tbsp. sugar
  2 Tbsps. water
  ½ lb. mascarpone cheese
  2 cups powdered sugar
2¾ cup heavy cream
 12 oz. bittersweet
     chocolate
  2 tsps. vanilla
  3 eggs
  1 cup milk
  3 Tbsps. butter, melted
  1 cup cornstarch
    Pinch of salt
    Parchment paper
    Chocolate shavings,
    garnish
    Sliced strawberries

THE WOODBOX INN

29 Fair Street
Nantucket, Massachusetts 02554
(508) 228-0587
ROOM RATES: $110–$180
AMENITIES: Nine rooms with fireplaces in the suites. Excellent restaurant on the premises, but breakfast is an additional charge. Short walk to the beach.
DIRECTIONS: From Straight Wharf, go up Main Street to Fair Street. Turn left to the inn.

Built in 1709, The Woodbox Inn is the oldest inn in Nantucket. The proud innkeepers of this establishment retain the colonial atmosphere of the old ship captain's house, decorating it with early-American antiques. Glowing brass candlesticks in the dining rooms, low-beamed ceilings, and pine-paneled walls add to the hospitable charm of this inn.

The Woodbox has nine units in all, including six suites with working fireplaces and one to two bedrooms in each.

The Woodbox Inn is a gourmet dining experience at breakfast and dinner.

Scampi Sauce

C ombine the shallots and garlic with oil in a saucepan for 2 minutes over medium-low heat. Add the Worcestershire sauce, sherry, lemon juice, and mustard. Bring to low boil for 5 minutes, remove from heat and add the butter and tarragon. Let sit until the butter has melted.

Before using, stir sauce with a wire whisk. Lemon juice and mustard help preserve this sauce in the refrigerator indefinitely.

To reheat, place in double boiler. Do not boil sauce after it has been made.

Trade Secret: You can substitute different mustards for various flavoring.

Yields: 2 Cups
Preparation Time:
   15 Minutes

   3 shallots
   2 cloves garlic
   1 Tbsp. olive oil
   2 Tbsps. Worcestershire
      sauce
      Salt to taste
   1 cup lemon juice
   1 cup sherry
   1 lb. butter
   ¾ cup Dijon mustard
   ¾ cup coarse ground
      mustard
   2 Tbsps. tarragon

VERMONT:
The Green
Mountain State

Although Vermont is sparsely populated (about 500,000 people and 2,400 dairy farms), the Green Mountain State has a lot to offer. It's a prime winter sports destination, with over 30 downhill skiing areas. Its spectacular fall foliage and over 100 covered bridges make it a photographer's dream.

Long noted for its maple sugar and syrup operations, Vermont also boasts a large cheese and dairy industry (Ben and Jerry's ice cream company is the industry's largest customer). So plentiful are quarried marble and granite that some towns even feature marble sidewalks.

Discovered by Samuel de Champlain in 1609, Vermont was under French control for nearly 150 years (the name comes from the French for green mountain). The British established a settlement in Brattleboro in 1724. But land claims by neighboring New York united Vermonters, with the formation in 1770 of the Green Mountain Boys militia, led by Ethan Allen. With the advent of the American Revolution, the militia joined the fight against England.

Vermont declared itself an independent republic in 1777. It had diplomatic relations with other countries, minted its own money and operated its own postal service. It became the 14th state of the union in 1791.

Here are some highlights of a trip to Vermont:

BRATTLEBORO — Site of Fort Dummer, a fortress built to repel the Indians. The Brattleboro Museum and Art Center, located in the old Union Railroad Station, is worth a stop. East of Brattleboro (the state is only 45 miles wide at this point) lies Marlboro, home of the Marlboro Music School and Festival, which was founded by Rudolf Serkin and was led by Pablo Casals for many years. Held every year in July and August, the festival seats only 700 people.

BENNINGTON — Residents boast that Bennington is "Vermont's most historic area." The town commemorates the Revolutionary War's battle of Benington, even though the battle site is in nearby New York state. Ethan Allen organized the Green Mountain Boys at the Catamount Tavern. Poet Robert Frost's grave is at the graveyard of the Old First Church. Frost's tombstone says, "I had a lover's quarrel with the world." Plan to visit three historic places: the Bennington Museum, the Bennington Battle Monument and the Park-McCullough House Museum. The museum contains many

☆

*A dapper fisherman
after a successful day in
Vermont.*

*Two stylish women
fly-fishing.*

*Photos from the
Vermont Historical Society.*

fine examples of Revolutionary and Early American artifacts. A highlight of the museum is its collection of Grandma Moses paintings. The Battle Monument is a 306-foot-tall stone obelisk, the tallest structure in Vermont. Visitors reach the top via an elevator. The Park-McCullough House, in North Bennington, an outstanding Victorian mansion, features wonderful period furniture and a miniature "manor" playhouse. North of Bennington, Arlington was home to famed artist Norman Rockwell. Over 1,000 reproductions of his work are displayed here.

MANCHESTER — There are three Manchesters: Manchester Center, Manchester Depot and Manchester Village. The story goes that Manchester Village in the early days was trying to attract tourists. Convinced that visitors would stay away from a town without sidewalks, the village took advantage of local marble quarries. The result: 17 miles of sidewalks made of marble. Manchester is also home to the Orvis Company, manufacturer of highly respected fishing rods and equipment. Fishermen will also want to visit the nearby American Museum of Fly Fishing, which displays over 1,500 rods, 800 reels 30,000 flies and the fishing tackle of many celebrities. The nearby town of Hildene contains the 24-room Georgian Revival home of Robert Todd Lincoln, son of Abraham Lincoln.

WOODSTOCK — This is the picturesque kind of town most visitors look for: a tree-lined village green, exquisite historic homes, a gentle stream flowing through town and a covered bridge. The town also boasts four church bells made by Paul Revere. Woodstock was the site of the first ski tow in the United States. In nearby Plymouth Notch, visit the Calvin Coolidge Homestead. U.S. Vice President Coolidge was visiting Plymouth in 1923 when he heard that President Harding had died. The oath of office was administered in Plymouth Notch by Coolidge's father, who was a local notary public. Also near Woodstock, look for the Raptor Center of the Vermont Institute of Natural Science. It houses 26 species of birds of prey. North of Montpelier, Stowe has an Alpine Slide. A chair lift takes you to the top of a mountain, where you board a small sled which you ride down a curving concrete runway to the bottom of the slope.

MONTPELIER — The state capital, Montpelier has a population of less than 9,000 people. The state capitol, modeled after the ancient Grecian Temple of Theseus, is made of local granite, with a gilded dome. The governor's chair is carved from wood from the frigate Constitution. Southeast of Montpelier is Barre (pronounced Berry), site of the Rock of Ages granite quarry, the world's largest. The local cemetery is quite a sight. Local stonecutters have gone out of their way to produce memorable granite monuments. Samples include self-portraits, a granite armchair and a husband and wife sitting up in bed.

BURLINGTON — Situated on the shore of Lake Champlain, Burlington (population 50,000) is Vermont's largest city. Long a trade center, the city is home to the University of Vermont. Nearby Shelburne is a must-see. The Shelburne Museum is a fascinating look into the past. Composed of 37 buildings on 45 acres, the museum includes a one-room schoolhouse, six early homes, an old-fashioned jail, a hunting lodge, a lighthouse, a 1920s carousel, a round barn and the 220-foot sidewheel steamship SS Ticonderoga. the complex has four art galleries and large displays of folk art.

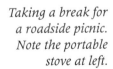

Taking a break for a roadside picnic. Note the portable stove at left.

BUTLER'S

ECLECTIC CUISINE
The Inn at Essex
70 Essex Way
Essex Junction, Vermont
(802) 879-5471
Dinner Monday–Saturday 6:00PM–10PM
AVERAGE DINNER FOR TWO: $50

Butler's is a fine dining restaurant located in the spacious Inn at Essex, a Georgian-style hotel. The food is prepared and served by second-year students of the New England Culinary Institute.

The menu features innovative food that is lively and flavorful, with a minimum of heavy sauces, butter or cream. Daily specials include beef, lamb, poultry, fish and vegetarian offerings.

The non-smoking restaurant is elegant and comfortable.

BUTLER'S MENU FOR FOUR

Crab Claws with Celery Root Remoulade

Salad Greens with Red Wine Vinaigrette

Stuffed Tenderloin

Vegetables in Smoked Tomato Ale Sauce

Hickory Smoked Salmon and Wild Rice with Vegetables

Frozen Margarita Parfait

Pears Poached in White Wine

Crab Claws
with Celery Root Remoulade

Blanch the carrot in boiling water for 1 minute, then immerse in cold water.

Combine the Dijon, mayonnaise, salt and pepper, celery root, pear and carrot. In a soup bowl, place 2 to 3 Tbsps. of the sauce. Arrange the crab claws, radicchio and lime wedges on the sauce and sprinkle with parsley.

Serves 4
Preparation Time:
 20 Minutes

2 Tbsps. carrot,
   julienned
4 Tbsps. Dijon mustard
1 cup mayonnaise
   Kosher salt to taste
   Pepper to taste
1 large celery root,
   peeled, thinly sliced,
   julienned
2 Tbsps. pear, julienned
8 small crab claws,
   cooked, cracked
8 leaves radicchio
1 lime, cut into
   16 wedges
   Chopped parsley for
   garnish

Salad Greens with Red Wine Vinaigrette

Serves 4
Preparation Time:
  10 Minutes

  1 cup red wine vinegar
    Kosher salt to taste
    Pepper to taste
  1 Tbsp. garlic, crushed
½ tsp. thyme
  1 Tbsp. red wine
  1 Tbsp. Worcestershire
    sauce
  1 cup corn oil
  1 cup olive oil
  1 lb. mixed salad greens

I n a mixing bowl, whisk together the vinegar, salt, pepper, garlic, thyme, wine and Worcestershire sauce.
Combine the oils and whisk into the vinegar mixture in a slow, steady stream. Season to taste.

Toss with salad greens. Season with salt and pepper and serve.

Stuffed Tenderloin

Sweat shallots in olive oil over medium heat. Add the greens and sauté until soft. Remove from heat, and salt and pepper to taste.

Cut a small hole in the side of each steak and hollow out a small pocket in the middle. Stuff each steak with the greens.

Grill steak to desired doneness. Grill bread until toasted. Serve each tenderloin on top of brioche.

Serves 4
Preparation Time:
  25 Minutes

  2 **shallots, sliced**
  4 **Tbsps. olive oil**
  ¼ **lb. spinach, cleaned**
  ¼ **lb. mustard greens,**
     cleaned
     Salt and pepper to
     taste
  4 **beef tenderloins, ½ lb.**
     each
  4 **slices brioche**

Vegetables in Smoked Tomato Ale Sauce

Serves 4
Preparation Time:
  20 Minutes
Cooking Time:
  1 Hour, 10 Minutes

1 **butternut squash,**
   peeled, ¼" diced
   Salt and sugar to taste
1 **turnip, peeled, cut into**
   12 wedges
1 **red bell pepper,**
   roasted, skinned
1 **red onion, julienned**
1 **cup chicken stock**
2 **tomatoes, roasted,**
   skinned, chopped
1½ **cups dark ale**
 ½ **lb. baby carrots**
   Olive oil

over the squash in a saucepan with cold water. Add salt and sugar to taste. Bring to a simmer for 5 minutes. Remove from heat and let cool.

Cover the turnip in a saucepan with cold water. Add salt and sugar to taste. Bring to a simmer. Remove from heat and steep for 20 minutes.

Purée the bell pepper in a blender. Set aside.

In a sauté pan, caramelize the red onions and deglaze with cold chicken stock. Add the tomatoes and the pepper purée. Simmer slowly for 45 minutes. Salt and pepper to taste. Add ale to taste. Once you add the ale do not reduce the sauce or it will become bitter. Strain the sauce.

Quickly sauté the squash, turnips and carrots in olive oil.

Serve the vegetables garnished with the sauce.

Smoked Salmon and Wild Rice with Onions, Asparagus and Baby Carrots

I n a large pan, sweat the shallots in 2 Tbsps. olive oil until they are translucent. Add the rice and coat the rice with oil. Add the cold water and bring to a boil. Add salt to taste and cook until the rice is tender.

In a mixing bowl, combine the onions with 4 Tbsps. olive oil, salt and pepper. On a hot grill, sear the onions on both sides. Set aside.

Wash the asparagus and plunge it into 2 qts. boiling, salted water. Cook until almost tender. Remove and cool in water.

Heat the carrots in 3 cups cold water with salt to taste, 1 Tbsp. sugar and butter. Bring to a boil and remove from heat. Let cool.

In a sauce pan, combine the Merlot with 2 Tbsps. sugar and the tarragon. Simmer slowly for 20 minutes. Add the cranberries and simmer 5 more minutes. Remove the tarragon stem from the sauce and liquefy the sauce in a blender. Strain.

Grill the salmon. Quickly sauté the vegetables to heat through.

To serve, place grilled salmon over a bed of rice. Surround with the grilled vegetables and drizzle the sauce over the top of the salmon.

Serves 4
Preparation Time:
  1 Hour
Cooking Time:
  35 Minutes

  1 shallot, sliced
  6 Tbsps. olive oil
  1 cup wild rice
  2 cups cold water
    Salt
  2 red onions, peeled,
    sliced ¼"
  ½ tsp. pepper
  2 bunches asparagus
  2 bunches baby carrots
  3 Tbsp. sugar
  2 Tbsps. butter
  ½ cup Merlot wine
  1 tarragon stem
  1 cup cranberries
  2 lbs. smoked salmon

☆

Frozen Margarita Parfait

Serves 4
Preparation Time:
 15 Minutes
(note refrigeration time)

  1 cup + 2 Tbsps.
     whipping cream
  3 egg yolks
3½ Tbsps. sugar
1½ Tbsps. honey
  6 Tbsps. sour mix
  5 Tbsps. Cuervo Gold
     tequila
 ½ Tbsp. Grand Marnier
  2 egg whites
     Oranges, strawberries
     or cookies for garnish

W hip cream to a soft peak and set aside.
        In a saucepan over a low flame, warm the egg yolks, 2 Tbsps. sugar and honey until dissolved. Remove from heat and transfer to a mixer. Blend until light and fluffy.

Whip the egg whites until firm, adding 1½ Tbsps. sugar slowly until the mix is stiff.

Combine the sour mix, tequila and Grand Marnier into the whipped cream, then fold this mixture into the yolk mixture. Finally, fold into the egg whites.

Spoon into timbales or glasses for freezing. Freeze until firm.

Garnish and serve.

Trade Secret: Use pasteurized eggs, as parfaits are not being cooked.

Pears Poached in White Wine

Combine all the ingredients, except the pears, and place in a saucepan over medium heat.
   While the liquid simmers, peel the pears, slice in half, core the middles.

Add the pears to the saucepan and cook slowly on a low heat. Simmer until the pears are tender, test by inserting a knife.

Cool and serve the pears with the juice.

Serves 4
Preparation Time:
   20 Minutes

   4 **cups white wine**
   ½ **cup water**
      Zest of one orange
      Zest of ½ lemon
   2 **Cinnamon sticks**
   ½ **cup honey**
   4 **peppercorns**
   3 **cloves**
   5 **pears, whole**

☆

Café Déjà Vu

GLOBAL CUISINE
185 Pearl Street
Burlington, Vermont
(802) 864-7917
Lunch and Dinner 11:30AM–11PM
AVERAGE DINNER FOR TWO: $30

O riginally designed as an elegant French-style crepery, the Café Déjà Vu now boasts a full international menu in exquisitely intimate surroundings. A series of rooms and a courtyard offer a sense of intimacy in this expansive restaurant. Cuisines to be sampled include American, French, Moroccan, Asian, Central and South American, Italian, Indian and Chinese, among others.

The eclectic menu from Chef Robert Fuller is a culinary delight featuring Cranberry Ginger Scallops, Vegetarian Crêpes with Sautéed Vegetables drizzled with a Cheddar and Tomato Wine Sauce, Grilled North African Chicken served with Couscous and Mint Yogurt and Escargots en Croute topped with a lattice of Puff Pastry and Artichokes.

CAFÉ DÉJÀ VU'S MENU FOR FOUR

Crabcakes with Mustard Caper Sauce

Sweet Potato Salad

Cranberry Ginger Scallops

Crab Cakes with Mustard Caper Sauce

I n a large bowl, combine the crabmeat, eggs, scallions, mayonnaise, baking powder, bread crumbs and lemon juice. Salt and pepper to taste. The consistency should be moist, so reserve some of the bread crumbs to adjust the moistness. Form the crab mixture into four patties as an appetizer or two patties as an entree. Refrigerate while preparing the sauce.

In a heavy saucepan over high heat, combine the wine, vermouth, shallots, salt and pepper. Reduce the sauce to 2 Tbsp. or less. Add the cream and reduce the volume in half until thickened.

Remove the saucepan from heat and slowly whisk in the butter. Stir in the mustard and capers. Season with salt and pepper.

Heat the olive oil in a medium-size skillet. Cook the crab cakes over medium heat until golden on both sides, about 3 minutes per side, adding more oil and butter as necessary.

Serve immediately with the mustard caper sauce.

Serves 4
Preparation Time:
  30 Minutes

  1 lb. fresh crabmeat
  2 eggs, lightly beaten
  2 scallions, chopped
  ½ cup mayonnaise
  ½ tsp. baking powder
  1 cup bread crumbs
  ½ tsp. lemon juice
    Salt and pepper to
    taste
  ½ cup white wine
  ¼ cup vermouth
  1 tsp. shallots, chopped
  ½ cup heavy cream
  ½ cup (1 stick) sweet
    butter
  1 Tbsp. grain mustard
  ½ Tbsp. capers, small
  1 Tbsp. olive oil

Sweet Potato Salad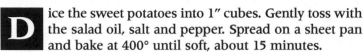

Serves 4
Preparation Time:
  25 Minutes
Cooking Time:
  15 Minutes

  2 lbs. sweet potatoes,
     peeled
  2 Tbsps. salad oil
     Salt and pepper to
     taste
  ¼ cup raspberry vinegar,
     (recipe follows on page
     189) or apple cider
     vinegar
  ¼ cup salad oil
  1 Tbsp. candied ginger,
     diced
  1 garlic clove, minced
  1 Tbsp. orange zest,
     diced
  2 Tbsps. orange juice
     concentrate
  ¼ cup pecans, chopped
  1 lb. mixed salad greens
     Garnish with raddichio
     or Belgian endive
  2 Tbsps. scallions,
     chopped
  2 Tbsps. cooked bacon,
     chopped, optional

D ice the sweet potatoes into 1" cubes. Gently toss with the salad oil, salt and pepper. Spread on a sheet pan and bake at 400° until soft, about 15 minutes.

Prepare the dressing by combining the vinegar, oil, ginger, garlic, orange zest, orange juice concentrate and pecans.

Toss the cooked sweet potatoes with the dressing and serve on a bed of salad greens. Garnish with raddichio lettuce or Belgian endive, scallions and bacon.

Trade Secret: This salad is wonderful served warm or cold.

★

Raspberry Vinegar

Combine the vinegar and 1 cup of the berries in a medium-size saucepan. Bring to a boil, then lower the heat and simmer, uncovered, for 2 minutes. Stir in the honey and remove from the heat.

Pour the berry mixture through a fine-mesh strainer into a large measuring cup. Don't press down on the berries. Discard the berries.

Divide the remaining 1 cup berries between two decorative, clean 16 oz. bottles. Pour the warm vinegar into the bottles.

Prepare at least one week in advance so that the flavors can infuse.

Yield: 1 quart
Preparation Time:
10 Minutes

1 qt. white vinegar
2 cups fresh raspberries
  or 6 oz. frozen berries,
  thawed
2 Tbsps. honey

★

Cranberry Ginger Scallops

Serves 4
Preparation Time:
20 Minutes

½ lb. sea scallops
   Flour to dust scallops
2 Tbsps. butter, melted
1 Tbsp. shallots, diced
¼ cup white wine
¾ cup cranberry chutney
   (recipe follows on
   page 191)
¼ cup heavy cream
1 Tbsp. candied ginger
   Orange zest

Rinse and dry scallops. Dust with flour just until dry. Set aside.

Heat a large sauté pan until very hot. Add the butter, then add the scallops in one layer. Cook on high heat and turn scallops when they are light brown, about 2 to 5 minutes.

Spoon the scallops onto a serving platter and place in a warm oven.

Add the shallots to the same sauté pan for 10 seconds. Add the wine and reduce by half. Add the cranberry chutney, cream and ginger. Reduce to desired sauce consistency and add the scallops back to the pan to re-heat.

Serve on warm plates and sprinkle with orange zest.

Trade Secret: This dish cooks very fast and must be cooked at the last minute. Have all the ingredients close at hand before you begin.

Cranberry Chutney

Stir all the ingredients thoroughly in a deep micro-wave-safe 1½-quart casserole. Cook, uncovered in a microwave at full power (650 to 700 watts) for 8 minutes. Stir, return to the microwave, and cook another 8 minutes.

Allow the chutney to cool slightly, then cover tightly and refrigerate for up to 2 days.

Yield: 2 cups
Preparation Time:
  25 Minutes

  1 12 oz. bag of
     cranberries
1½ cups brown sugar
  ¼ lime, chopped
  ⅓ lemon, chopped
  1 tsp. cinnamon
  1 Tbsp. candied ginger
  ½ tsp. black pepper,
     coarsely ground

THE MIDDLEBROOK RESTAURANT

FRESH LOCAL CUISINE
Middlebrook Road
Fairlee, Vermont
(802) 333-4240
Dinner Wednesday–Sunday 5PM–9PM
AVERAGE DINNER FOR TWO: $30

L ocated on 115 acres of beautiful, rolling Vermont countryside, corn and alfalfa fields, woodland, and their own vegetable and flower gardens, the Middlebrook Restaurant creates an exceptional environment for relaxed dining.

Built by the owners, the restaurant is designed to replace the original barn which was removed in the 1940s, with playful and dramatic elements added to the country charm.

The food is fresh and eclectic; Chef John Quimby draws upon the European tradition of a small menu that changes daily to reflect the seasons and the region's specialties. The meals are interesting and creative in a relaxed country setting.

Guests can taste such local samples as Strudel of Smoked Salmon and Leeks, Grilled Swordfish with Cilantro Lime Pesto and Almonds, Duck Breast with Fresh Figs and Marsala, Herb Pasta Torta with Spring Greens and Cheddar or Roasted Cumin Garlic Pork in a Tomato Pepper Sauce.

THE MIDDLEBROOK RESTAURANT'S MENU FOR SIX

Salmon and Asparagus Chowder

Cheddar and Dill Biscuits

Salad Greens with Chive Blossom Dijon Vinaigrette

Salmon and Asparagus Chowder

I n a large heavy-bottomed pot, gently cook the bacon, or melt butter. When the bacon begins to brown, add the diced onion. Continue cooking on low heat, stirring frequently, until the onion is transparent. Add the minced garlic and stir for 15 seconds. Add the cream. When the cream begins to simmer, add the potatoes. Simmer until tender, stirring occasionally. Add the asparagus and simmer 2 minutes. Add the salmon, stir once and remove from heat. Salt and pepper to taste. After 3 minutes, the salmon cubes should be poached perfectly, and should still retain their shape.

Serve immediately.

Trade Secret: Salmon tails are excellent for this preparation, less expensive and boneless. This soup cooks quickly, so have all ingredients cleaned and cut prior to cooking.

Serves 6
Preparation Time:
  15 Minutes

¼ lb. bacon slices, cut into ¼" strips (4 Tbsps. butter can be substituted for bacon)
2 medium onions, peeled, diced
1 garlic clove, minced
1 qt. heavy cream
4 red potatoes, quartered, cut into ¼" slices
1 lb. asparagus, peeled, cut into ¼" diagonal slices, tips left whole
1 lb. fresh boneless salmon filet, cut into ½" cubes
Salt and pepper to taste

Cheddar and Dill Biscuits

Serves 6
Preparation Time:
   10 Minutes
Baking Time:
   15 Minutes

   6 **Tbsps. (¾ stick) butter,**
      cold, cubed
   2 **cups all-purpose flour**
   1 **Tbsp. baking powder**
   1 **tsp. salt**
   ¼ **tsp. pepper**
   1 **Tbsp. fresh dill, finely**
      chopped
   ½ **cup sharp cheddar**
      cheese, grated
   ¾ **cup milk**

Cut the butter into the flour, in a food processor. Add the remaining ingredients to the food processor and pulse quickly several times, until the butter is in small pieces. Do not over-mix.

If mixing by hand, cut the butter into the dry ingredients with two knives or a pastry cutter. Add the milk and stir quickly.

The dough should be stiff and just moist enough to hold together. With two soup spoons, form even-sized balls and drop onto ungreased baking pan. The dough will be bumpy.

Bake on the top oven shelf at 375° for 10 to 15 minutes or until browned on top. Serve hot.

Salad Greens with
Chive Blossom Dijon Vinaigrette

P lace the mustard in a small bowl. Whisk in the vinegar. Slowly whisk in the olive oil, until mixture is smooth and creamy. Adjust consistency, if desired, with vinegar or oil.

Add the chopped chives and flowerettes. Reserve a few flowers for garnishing. Salt and pepper to taste.

Toss dressing with salad greens.

Trade Secret: Chive flowers taste wonderful and are a beautiful visual addition to many dishes. They have a mild garlicky-onion flavor and an unusual lavender color. Freshly opened flowers are best; older ones are papery. For most foods, cut the flower head from the base and husk that hold the flower. Flower stems are not recommended for eating, unlike the hollow tender leaf stalks normally used.

Serves 6
Preparation Time:
  10 Minutes

  3 **Tbsps. Dijon mustard**
  ¼ **cup white wine**
     vinegar
  1 **cup olive oil**
  2 **Tbsps. chives, finely**
     chopped
  2 **Tbsps. chive**
     flowerettes
     Salt and pepper to
     taste
  1 **lb. mixed salad greens**

★

THE PRINCE & THE PAUPER

CONTINENTAL CUISINE
24 Elm Street
Woodstock, Vermont
(802) 457-1818
Dinner 6PM–11PM
AVERAGE DINNER FOR TWO: $60

An intimate dining experience, The Prince & The Pauper is located in the heart of Woodstock. The bar invites patrons to relax among dark woods and enjoy the house specialty cheese spread. The dining room takes visitors back in time with wooden booths and old prints on the walls, dark beams on the ceiling and oil lamps at every table.

The $30 prix fixe menu changes with the seasons, and can include chef/owner Chris Balcer's famous dishes such as Pasta cooked with Smoked Ham, Mushrooms, Tomatoes and Cream, a Seared Veal Rib Chop with Sautéed Spinach, Pancetta and Fontina Cheese, Broiled Filet of Maine Salmon and a Indonesian Lamb Curry braised with aromatic Vegetables over Rice Pilaf with Mango chutney.

THE PRINCE & THE PAUPER'S MENU FOR FOUR

Mousseline of Three Salmon

Garden Salad with Tomato-Herb Vinaigrette

Asparagus and Sorrel Vichyssoise

Rack of Lamb Royale

Roast Chicken with Morels

Steamed New Potatoes

Bourbon Pecan Cheesecake

Mousseline of Three Salmon

Cut salmon filet into 1" pieces and place in a food processor. Add salt, pepper and brandy. Mix to form a smooth purée, scraping sides of the bowl once. Add egg whites one at a time while continuing to purée salmon. Scrape the bowl once more. Put the mixture in a chilled bowl.

Whip 1 cup heavy cream into soft peaks. With a rubber spatula, fold the cream into the salmon mixture a little at a time, combining well.

Spoon ⅓ of the mixture into a well-buttered loaf pan approximately 9"×4"×3".

Arrange ½ of the smoked salmon slices over the top of the mousseline. Repeat this step again and top with the remaining mousseline. Place pan in a water bath and bake at 350° for 35 to 45 minutes. Mousseline is done when meat thermometer reads 150°.

Let cool 30 minutes. Gently turn mousseline onto a plate and chill overnight.

When ready to serve, whip 2 cups chilled heavy cream into soft peaks. Fold in horseradish, lemon and Worcestershire.

Carefully slice ½" pieces of mousse onto chilled plates. Arrange a dollop of cream sauce alongside mousse and sprinkle a teaspoon of roe over the sauce. You may wish to garnish with capers, sliced onion, parsley or lemon wedges.

Serves 4
Preparation Time:
  30 Minutes
Cooking Time:
  45 Minutes

1½ lbs. salmon filets,
    boneless, skinned
  2 tsps. salt
 ½ tsp. white pepper
  1 Tbsp. brandy
  4 egg whites
  3 cups heavy cream
 ⅓ lb. smoked salmon,
    thinly sliced
  1 Tbsp. horseradish
  1 tsp. lemon juice
 ½ tsp. Worcestershire
    sauce
  1 oz. caviar or salmon
    roe

Garden Salad
with Tomato-Herb Vinaigrette

Serves 4
Preparation Time:
  15 Minutes

  1 lb. mixed garden
    greens
  1 cup olive oil
  1 Tbsp. lemon juice
  2 tsps. sugar
  1 tsp. salt
  1 tomato, skinned,
    seeded
  4 fresh basil leaves (or
    1 tsp. dried)
  ½ tsp. white pepper
  2 tsps. Dijon mustard,
    optional

 ash and dry greens.
    Place the remaining ingredients in a blender and
purée until smooth.
Pour vinaigrette over salad and serve.

★

Asparagus and Sorrel Vichyssoise

Discard the white ends of the asparagus and chop the remaining stalks.

Trim the leeks, saving the white bottoms. Wash leeks thoroughly and chop.

Peel the potato and cut into 1" cubes.

In a heavy saucepan, melt the butter over medium heat. Add the leeks and asparagus and gently sauté for 10 minutes until lightly browned. Reduce the heat and add the flour. Cook for 5 minutes more, stirring occasionally. Add the stock and bring to a boil. Add the potatoes and simmer about 15 minutes. Add the cream and simmer another 5 minutes. Remove the soup from heat. Salt and pepper to taste.

Add the sorrel leaves to the soup and purée in a blender. Remove and strain through a sieve.

Serve warm or chilled. Garnish with chopped chives if desired.

Serves 4
Preparation Time:
 45 Minutes

- 1 lb. asparagus
- 2 leeks
- 1 medium potato
- 2 Tbsps. butter
- 2 Tbsps. flour
- 4 cups vegetable or chicken stock
- 1 cup heavy cream
  Salt and pepper to taste
- ¼ cup sorrel leaves, chopped
  Chives, chopped, optional

Rack of Lamb Royale

Serves 4
Preparation Time:
  45 Minutes
(note refrigeration time)
Cooking Time:
  30 Minutes

  2 **lamb racks, eight-ribs**
    each
  1 **lb. fresh spinach leaves**
  ¾ **lb. mushroom caps**
  ¼ **cup clarified butter**
  ¼ **cup shallots, minced**
  ½ **tsp. fresh thyme**
  2 **cups Zinfandel wine**
    Salt and pepper to
    taste
  1 **cup demi-glacé**
  4 **puff pastry sheets**
    3"×9"

emove the rib eye from each lamb rack (reserve) and cut into 2 equal pieces, or ask the butcher to prepare them.

Remove the stems from the spinach and wash the leaves. Blanch the spinach leaves in boiling water, rinse in cold water, press out the water, chop spinach and chill.

Mince the mushrooms in a food processor or finely chop. Heat ½ of the clarified butter in a sauté pan and sauté half the shallots until lightly brown. Add the mushrooms, thyme and salt and pepper to taste. Cook over medium heat until the mushrooms are brown and liquid evaporates. Add 1 cup of red wine and continue to cook until all wine is evaporated. Chill the mushroom mixture.

Heat the remaining butter in a sauté pan. Brown the boneless lamb rib eyes over medium heat for 4 minutes on each side. Remove the lamb. In the same pan, sauté the remaining shallots until lightly brown. Add the remaining wine and continue to cook until all of the wine is evaporated. Add the demi-glacé and simmer for 15 minutes.

While the sauce is simmering, spoon the mushroom mixture onto the center of the puff pastry sheets. Top the mushroom mixture with the chopped spinach. Top the spinach with a piece of lamb. Pull one end of the puff pastry up over the top of the lamb and repeat with the other end. overlapping by ½". Press the seam shut and arrange on a baking sheet, seam side down. Bake 15 to 20 minutes at 450° until the puff pastry is golden brown.

Slice into 3 medallions. Place warm sauce on each plate and arrange lamb medallions over sauce.

★

Roast Chicken with Morels

Remove the neck and giblets from the chicken's body cavity. Rinse and pat the chicken dry. Season inside of chicken with rosemary.

Gently loosen the skin from top and sides of breast and place half the morels between the skin and breast meat.

Mix together the chopped onion, carrots and celery. Place half of this mixture in a roasting pan large enough to hold the chicken.

Place the other half in a saucepan with the neck, giblets and last joint of the chicken wings. Cover with cold water and add the bay leaf. Simmer gently for 1½ hours.

Meanwhile, place the chicken in the roasting pan, season with salt and pepper. Roast at 350° for 18 minutes per pound, 1½ to 1¾ hours.

Remove the chicken to a platter and let stand in a warm place for 15 minutes.

Strain the chicken stock from the saucepan into the roasting pan and add the remaining morels. Reduce the liquid over high heat, scraping the bottom and sides of the roasting pan. When the stock is reduced to 2 cups, strain the liquid and reserve.

Carve chicken onto serving plates and moisten with juice.

Serves 4
Preparation Time:
  45 Minutes
Cooking Time:
  1 Hour, 45 Minutes

  1 **roasting chicken, 5 to 6 lbs.**
  1 **tsp. rosemary**
  ¼ **cup fresh morel mushrooms, sliced**
  2 **onions, finely chopped**
  2 **carrots, finely chopped**
  2 **celery stalks, finely chopped**
  6 **cups cold water**
  1 **bay leaf**
  1 **tsp. salt**
  ½ **tsp. white pepper**

☆

Steamed New Potatoes

Serves 4
Preparation Time:
  10 Minutes
Cooking Time:
  30 Minutes

  1 **lb. new potatoes**
  2 **Tbsps. butter, unsalted**
  2 **tsps. fresh dill,**
     chopped

Wash potatoes. Arrange in a large strainer basket and place over a boiling pot of shallow water. Cover and cook 30 minutes or until potatoes can be easily pierced with a fork. When done, gently toss potatoes with dill and butter.

Bourbon Pecan Cheesecake

Warm the cream cheese to room temperature. Beat the cheese, adding the four eggs one at a time. Add the yolk and beat until smooth. Slowly add ¾ cup sugar and the bourbon. Beat until light, scraping the bottom of the bowl. Stir in the flour.

Combine the graham cracker crumbs, 3 Tbsps. melted butter and 3 Tbsps. sugar with a fork.

Press the mixture evenly into a 10" springform cake pan.

For the topping, place the brown sugar in a small bowl. Add the remaining butter and cut until mixture resembles a coarse meal. Stir pecans into mixture.

Pour the batter into the cake pan. Bake at 325° for about 1½ hours, or until the center no longer moves when the pan is shaken. Sprinkle the topping over the cake and bake 15 minutes more. Refrigerate overnight.

Trade Secret: If you do not wish to use alcohol, substitute 1 Tbsp. lemon juice and 1 tsp. vanilla extract for the bourbon.

Serves 12
Preparation Time:
  30 Minutes
Baking Time:
  1 Hour, 45 Minutes
(note refrigeration time)

2½ lbs. cream cheese
 4 eggs
 1 egg yolk
 1 cup sugar
 3 Tbsps. bourbon
 2 Tbsps. all-purpose
   flour
 2 cups graham cracker
   crumbs
 9 Tbsps. (1⅛ sticks)
   melted butter
 ¾ cup brown sugar
1½ cups pecans, chopped

☆

KEDRON VALLEY INN

Route 106
South Woodstock, Vermont 05071
(802) 457-1473
ROOM RATES: $119–$191
AMENITIES: Thirty rooms with bath, many with fireplace or wood stove, breakfast included, restaurant, lounge, reception/meeting facilities, pond with beach, horseback riding, sleigh and surrey rides, 15-acre grounds, near downhill and cross-country skiing.
DIRECTIONS: From I-91, take Exit 8 onto Hwy. 131 West. Turn right (north) at the blinking light onto Route 106. The inn is 13.6 miles, on the left. From I-89, take Hwy. 4 West from White River Jct., then turn left (south) onto Route 106 in Woodstock. The inn is 5 miles, on the right.

K edron Valley Inn is one of Vermont's oldest, having originated as a private home and inn in 1828. In 1840, it became the National Hotel, a social center with ballroom and carriage entrance. Every room is graced with a family quilt from the innkeepers, each with its own history handwritten beside it. Antique rocking chairs, canopy beds, and other decorations give the inn its authentic country charm. Owners Max and Merrily Comins began renovating the inn in 1985, and it has since become a top draw for tourists to the area.

This inn offers activities and majestic scenery in all seasons, as well as fabulous food in the restaurant. Chef Tom Hopewell creates what he calls "Nouvelle Vermont" cuisine such as Oven Roasted Mediterranean Ravioli, Baked Escargot in New Potatoes, Confit of Duck Salad, Tournedos of Venison, Filet of Salmon Poached with Fumet and Champagne, and the day's fresh pastries.

Salmon in a Puff Pastry with Seafood Mousse

Cut salmon into four 4-oz. filets. Save one 2-oz. piece for the mousse. Slice each filet in half lengthwise, so that one piece can be placed on top of the mousse on the other piece.

Put 2-oz. piece of salmon, shrimp and scallops in a very cold bowl of a blender or food processor. Pulse a little to mix. Slowly add the heavy cream and egg white while blending, for about 1 minute. Remove to another bowl. Add the herbs and pepper to the mixture and gently fold.

Place the bottom half of the salmon on a puff pastry. Place 3 to 4 Tbsps. of mousse on the salmon and cover with the top half. Bring four corners of the pastry together on top and squeeze to secure. Repeat with remaining filets and pastries.

Beat egg with milk.

Lightly butter a baking pan and place pastries, seam sides down, on the pan. Brush each one with the egg wash. Bake at 425° for about 7 minutes until golden brown. Remove and let stand 2 to 3 minutes.

Trade Secret: Kedron Valley Chef Tom Hopewell recommends a good Chardonnay and assorted fresh vegetables with this dish.

Serves 4
Preparation Time:
  30 Minutes
Cooking Time:
  10 Minutes

1 salmon filet, 18 oz.
¼ lb. shrimp, raw, peeled, deveined
¼ lb. sea scallops
1 cup heavy cream
1 egg white
1 tsp. chives
1 tsp. tarragon
1 tsp. parsley
¼ tsp. white pepper
4 puff pastry squares, 5"×5"
1 egg
1 Tbsp. milk

WEST MOUNTAIN INN

Route 313, River Road
Arlington, Vermont 05250
(802) 375-6516
ROOM RATES: $160–$180
AMENITIES: Fifteen rooms, three suites with kitchens, many with views and fireplaces, 150-acre wooded grounds. Breakfast and six-course dinner inclusive. Near cross-country skiing, canoeing, hiking, trout fishing.
DIRECTIONS: Take Route 7 north from Bennington to the Arlington Exit. Follow signs to Route 313. Take Route 313 about one mile to the inn on the left.

Originally an 1849 farmhouse, the spacious West Mountain Inn reigns on a hill overlooking the Battenkill River and village of Arlington. The peaceful philosophies of owners Wes and Mary Ann Carlson are reflected in every touch, from the African violets, fruit and trail maps awaiting guests in each room to the llamas and wildlife present on the grounds. Wes breeds the llamas and raises the violets himself, giving away over 2,000 of the flowers each year. The Carlsons describe the inn as "a place where people go to relax, revitalize and affirm their affection for one another."

West Mountain Eggs and Béarnaise Sauce

For the béarnaise sauce: Beat the egg yolks, lemon juice, tarragon and vinegar. Transfer the mixture to a double boiler. Over low heat, stir constantly until sauce thickens. The water in the double boiler should simmer, but not boil.

Remove from heat and beat in the butter, salt and cayenne pepper. Keep warm.

Split and toast the English muffins.

Place a tomato slice on each muffin half. Place the spinach on top of tomato.

Boil water in a large pot. Crack the eggs into the pot and poach 3 minutes.

Place an egg on each muffin half, on top of the spinach. Top with béarnaise sauce and paprika.

©"Folk and Fare"

Serves 4
Preparation Time:
  10 Minutes

  8 **egg yolks**
  2 **Tbsps. lemon juice**
1½ **tsps. tarragon**
  2 **Tbsps. + ½ tsp.**
     tarragon vinegar
  1 **lb. butter, melted**
     Salt and cayenne
     pepper to taste
  4 **English muffins**
  2 **medium tomatoes,**
     sliced
 ½ **lb. spinach leaves,**
     cooked
1½ **qts. water**
  8 **eggs**
     Paprika

Applesauce Bread

Yield: 2 loaves
Preparation Time:
  10 Minutes
Cooking Time:
  1 Hour

  1 cup (2 sticks)
    margarine
  1 cup sugar
  2 eggs
  1 cup raisins
 ⅔ cup nuts, chopped
  4 cups flour
  4 tsps. baking soda
1½ tsps. cinnamon
 ½ tsp. cloves
  1 tsp. salt
  3 cups applesauce

C ream the margarine and sugar together in a mixing bowl. Add the eggs.

In a separate bowl, combine the dry ingredients. Add the dry ingredients to the egg mixture. Mix thoroughly. Stir in applesauce.

Grease and flour 2 loaf pans and fill ⅔ full.

Bake at 350° until done, about 50 to 60 minutes.

©"Folk and Fare"

Glazed Beets

Slice or halve the beets. Set aside.

Heat a sauté pan. Blend the sugar, salt and cornstarch in the pan. Add the vinegar and beet juice. Mix well until thickened, stirring constantly, about 5 minutes. Add the beets and butter. Cook on low heat about 10 minutes.

Serve hot.

©"Folk and Fare"

Serves 6
Preparation Time:
  20 Minutes

  3 lbs. beets, fresh or
     canned, cooked,
     peeled
  ⅓ cup sugar
  ½ tsp. salt
  1 Tbsp. cornstarch
  ½ cup cider vinegar
  ½ cup beet juice
  2 Tbsps. butter

NEW HAMPSHIRE:
The Model
of Democracy

Most people think of New Hampshire in the context of presidential elections — the first election returns always come from Dixville Notch, N.H. The reason? The polling place (for about 34 voters) is at the Balsams Grand Resort Hotel, which has its own phone system. So there's never any trouble getting the word out.

But New Hampshire has a lot more going for it. With an ocean coastline of 18 miles, it still boasts six state parks and beaches in that space. It is the home of the famed Old Man of the Mountain, 54 covered truss bridges, 1,300 lakes, the second-most climbed mountain in the world, and was the site of the movie,"On Golden Pond."

And the state has no earned-income tax or retail sales tax. Its government is financed by property taxes, taxes on liquor, restaurant meals and lodging, and a state lottery.

New Hampshire's House of Representatives is the largest state assembly in the country, with 400 members. Every town with a large-enough population sends at least one representative to Concord, the state capital.

Called the Granite State, New Hampshire's motto came from Revolutionary War hero General John Stark: "Live free or die."

First exploration of the state by Europeans was recorded in 1603. But there is evidence that Norsemen landed in New Hampshire in the 11th century.

Here are some highlights of a visit to New Hampshire:

HAMPTON BEACH — This seaside resort features a three-mile-long boardwalk. Nearby Hampton contains many historic buildings and a historic puzzle. Norseman's Rock is marked with runic characters that suggest that Norsemen visited Hampton around the year 1000. Local legend had it that Leif Ericson's brother, Thorvald, was buried under the rock. But scientists have not been able to to find a trace of the Viking's body. A little south of Hampton lies Seabrook, home of an aquarium and a nuclear power plant.

PORTSMOUTH — Further north on the Atlantic coast lies Portsmouth, former state capital and the state's major seaport. It contains the Strawberry Banke outdoor museum, a ten-acre section of buildings, some dating from 1695. The area is filled with craftspeople who show how chairs, tables and cabinets were made. You'll also learn about shipbuilding. Other Portsmouth attractions include many historic man-

A policeman directs traffic in front of Chick's Lunch Room.

Rodolphe Blais, proud manager of the People's Market on Daniels Street.

Photos from Strawberry Banke Museum.

sions and houses, such as the John Paul Jones home, now home to the Portsmouth Historical Society. The Port of Portsmouth Maritime Museum is home to the *U.S.S. Albacore*, a prototype submarine built in 1953.

MANCHESTER — If you like to hunt for bargains, Manchester is the place for you. The largest city in New Hampshire contains dozens of factory outlet stores (there are more in North Conway and other towns). Also worth seeing is Amoskeag Mills, which extend for a mile along the Merrimack River. South of Manchester are two intriguing stops: Merrimack, the home of the Clydesdale draft horses; and Salem, America's version of Stonehenge. Large monoliths of stone (smaller than England's) were carefully positioned to coincide with lunar and solar alignments. Some speculate that one flat stone was used for human sacrifices. Celtic and Iberian inscriptions indicate that a mysterious culture thrived in Salem around 4,000 years ago.

CONCORD — The state capital since 1816, Concord was first settled in 1725, when it was called Rumsford. The State House, built in 1819, is one of the nation's oldest. Naturally, it is built of granite and marble. You may want to make time for a trip to Canterbury, north of Concord. This is home to an original Shaker village, which was established circa 1780. Guided tours explain how men and women lived apart and how the Shakers made furniture that is still prized today.

LAKE WINNIPESAUKEE — Its name means "Smile of the Great Spirit." The popular lake, 28 miles long, contains about 300 islands. The lake is popular with summer vacationers. On the northern end of Lake Winnipesaukee is Castle in the Clouds, a lavish stone castle built by eccentric millionaire Thomas Plant. Nearby is Squam Lake, where "On Golden Pond" was filmed.

MONADNOCK MOUNTAIN — Situated in the southern part of the state, this National Natural Landmark rises 3,165 feet above the plain. It is the country's most-climbed mountain, second in the world only to Japan's Mount Fuji.

OLD MAN OF THE MOUNTAIN — This natural granite formation is found in Franconia Notch State Park. The 40-foot face, situated 1,000 feet above the valley floor, is a big attraction. Nathaniel Hawthorne wrote about it and there is ☆ even talk that showman P.T. Barnum wanted to buy it.

A peanut stand in front of Joseph Dondero's store.

The Holland Market was established in 1890.

BLUE STRAWBERRY

AMERICAN CUISINE
29 Ceres Street
Portsmouth, New Hampshire
(603) 431-6420
Dinner seating nightly 7:30PM
AVERAGE DINNER FOR TWO: $84

Relaxed, warm and comfortable, Blue Strawberry is housed in a 1797 restored ship's chandlery warehouse overlooking Portsmouth's historical harbor. A variety of antique chairs, china, silverware and crystal add to the candlelit surroundings of brick walls and beamed ceilings. The highly rated restaurant is a local favorite.

The menu changes daily, and all foods are freshly prepared for the 7:30 evening seating by confirmed reservation only. All guests are served the six-course dinner family-style at a fixed price of $42 per person.

Owners Philip McGuire and Gene Brown opened the restaurant in 1970. Philip is the chef and often offers such samples as Phyllo Pastry Stuffed with Spiced Pork, Snails Baked in Garlic Scotch Whisky Butter, Tenderloin of Beef Wellington in Gingered Madeira Wine and Mushroom Sauce, and Fresh Strawberries with Brown Sugar and Sour Cream.

BLUE STRAWBERRY'S MENU FOR EIGHT

Sweet and Sour Raspberry Vinaigrette

Curry Tomato Cream Soup Topped with Sherry and Corn

Roasted Duck and Poblano Chile Puff Pastry on Red Pepper Purée

Roasted Leg of Lamb in Mint, Garlic, Port Wine and Mushroom Sauce

Sweet and Sour Raspberry Vinaigrette

P lace the garlic, onion, brown sugar, mustard, salt and pepper in a blender. Add the Chambord and vinegar. With the blender running, add the oil slowly. If dressing becomes too thick, add a spoonful of cold water.

Toss the lettuce lightly with the vinaigrette. Serve immediately.

Serves 8
Preparation Time:
   10 Minutes

   3 garlic cloves, crushed
   1 small onion, finely
      chopped
   1 Tbsp. brown sugar
   1 Tbsp. Dijon mustard
      Salt and pepper to
      taste
   ½ cup Chambord liqueur
   ¾ cup raspberry vinegar
   3 cups olive oil
   1 lb. fresh salad greens

Curry Tomato Cream Soup Topped with Sherry and Corn

Serves 8
Preparation Time:
 40 Minutes

 2 small potatoes, peeled,
   diced
 3 garlic cloves
 1 leek, cleaned, chopped
 1 small green bell
   pepper, roasted,
   seeded
 4 cups chicken stock
 1 28-oz. can tomatoes
 1 small can tomato
   paste
 2 Tbsps. curry powder
 1 pt. light cream
 1 qt. milk
   Salt and white pepper
   to taste
 2 ears corn, kernels cut
   off
 1 Tbsp. butter
 ½ cup dry sherry
   Watercress for garnish

I n a soup pot, combine the potatoes, garlic, leeks and bell pepper with the chicken stock. Simmer until potatoes are soft. Add the tomatoes, tomato paste, curry, cream and half the milk. Salt and pepper to taste.

Return to a simmer, adding more milk if the soup begins to look too thick. Adjust the seasonings to taste. Do not let the soup boil or it will curdle.

In a sauté pan melt the butter and sauté the corn until just cooked, about 2 minutes. Add the sherry and a little salt and pepper. Heat to a simmer.

Pour the soup into individual soup bowls. Top each bowl with a spoonful of the corn and sherry. Garnish with a sprig of watercress.

Roasted Duck and Poblano Chile Puff Pastry on Sweet Red Pepper Purée

Place duck, skin side up, on a roasting pan. Prick the skin all over to allow the fat to cook off. Rub salt, pepper and paprika into the skin and place the duck in the oven at 400° for about 30 minutes. The skin should be golden-brown and crisp, and the breast meat medium-rare. Remove from the oven and let cool.

When cool, discard any uncooked fat. Save the crisp, cooked skin. Slice all the meat and skin together in a bowl. Mix in the chile sauce, goat cheese and capers.

Place diced red pepper, tomatoes, garlic, dashes of salt, pepper and maple syrup, and tomato paste in a food processor. Blend until smooth. Chill until ready to use.

Unroll the puff pastry sheets and cut into 2" strips. Roll out strip with a rolling pin until length is increased by ⅓. Cut strips into thirds.

On each puff pastry, lay one strip of poblano chile in the middle and cover with the duck mixture. Place another strip of chile on top and roll up pastry. Make about 2 per person.

Brush beaten egg on the top of the pastry.

Bake at 375° for about 15 minutes or until puffed up and golden brown.

Serve on a pool of the pepper purée. Garnish with scallion slivers.

Serves 8
Preparation Time:
 45 Minutes
Cooking Time:
 45 Minutes

1 duck, 4 lbs., excess fat
  trimmed
  Salt and pepper to
  taste
  Paprika to taste
1 Tbsp. Thai chile sauce
2 oz. goat cheese
2 Tbsps. capers
3 red bell peppers,
  roasted, skinned,
  seeded, diced
4 Italian tomatoes,
  skinned, seeded (fresh
  or canned)
4 garlic cloves, roasted,
  or microwave-steamed
  for 30 seconds
  Maple syrup to taste
1 Tbsp. tomato paste
2 sheets puff pastry
6 poblano chiles,
  roasted, cut 2"×½"
1 egg, beaten
  Scallion slivers for
  garnish

★

Roasted Leg of Lamb in Mint, Garlic, Port Wine and Mushroom Sauce

Serves 8
Preparation Time:
  45 Minutes
(note refrigeration time)
Cooking Time:
  2 Hours, 30 Minutes

  1 **whole leg of lamb, 6 to
     7 lbs.**
  6 **garlic cloves, minced**
  1 **bunch fresh mint
     Salt and pepper to
     taste**
  2 **Tbsps. olive oil
     Port Wine Plum
     Tomato Sauce (recipe
     follows on page 219)**

T ake the bones out of the lamb, remove the fat and skin. Reserve bones.

Mix the garlic, mint, a teaspoon of salt and pepper and the olive oil. Coat the lamb with the garlic mint mixture. Refrigerate at least 4 hours.

Roast the lamb at 450° for 10 minutes. Turn upside down and roast for another 10 minutes. Reduce heat to 375° and roast for 30 minutes more. Lamb is rare to medium when internal meat thermometer reads 130°. Remove the lamb from the oven and let rest 15 to 20 minutes, then carve.

Port Wine Plum Tomato Sauce

oast the lamb bones in the oven at 400° for 20 to 30 minutes. Deglaze the roasting pan with some of the beef stock.

Mix cornstarch with 1 tsp. port wine. Set aside.

Remove the bones to a saucepan. Cover with the rest of the beef stock and port wine. Add about 1 cup of water if needed to cover the bones. Simmer covered for 1 hour.

Carefully strain this stock into another saucepan. Discard the bones. Skim off any fat from the sauce and add the plum tomatoes with juice, the mushrooms and the leek. Simmer until reduced by half. Add pepper and a little balsamic vinegar to taste. Add the cornstarch mixture. Add salt if needed.

Keep warm until ready to serve over lamb.

Yield: 1½ cups
Preparation Time:
  15 Minutes
Cooking Time:
  1 Hour, 30 Minutes

  Bones from the lamb
2 cups beef stock
1 tsp. cornstarch
1 cup port wine
1 can Italian plum
  tomatoes
1 lb. small white
  mushrooms
1 medium leek,
  ½″ slices
  Salt and pepper to
  taste
  Balsamic vinegar

D'ARTAGNAN

FRENCH-STYLE CUISINE
13 Dartmouth College Hwy.
Lyme, New Hampshire
(603) 795-2137
Lunch Sunday 12PM–1:15PM
Dinner Wednesday–Sunday 6PM–9:15PM
DINNER FOR TWO: $76 prix fixe

Sumptuous French food in a landscaped historic park characterizes the richness of D'Artagnan. Just north of Dartmouth College, the restaurant resides in an eighteenth-century brick tavern overlooking a tree-lined stream.

Chefs/owners Peter Gaylor and Rebecca Cunningham have impeccable training in French cuisine, Gaylor having studied in France and both having been chefs for Yannick Cam, formerly of Le Pavillon in Washington, D.C. Nonetheless, D'Artagnan's atmosphere is simple and casual. They require neither a dress code nor fluent French to order from the menu.

The menu from D'Artagnan includes Soup of Acorn and Blue Hubbard Squash, Pâté of Pheasant with Cognac, Pan Roasted Vermont Rabbit with Watercress, Sautéed Filet of Salmon on Confit of Cabbage, and Roast Rack of Lamb with Tomato Rosemary Sauce.

Rebecca Cunningham's sumptuous dessert menu features Terrine of Dark Chocolate with Mocha Sauce, Apples stuffed with Currants and Pecans in a Pastry with Vanilla Ice Cream, and a Sorbet of Three Fruits with Cointreau.

D'ARTAGNAN'S MENU FOR EIGHT

Salad of Venison with a Walnut Vinaigrette

Pan Roasted Rabbit with Mustard Sauce

Pear Almond Cream Tart

Salad of Venison with a Walnut Vinaigrette

repare the vinaigrette in a mixing bowl by combining the shallots, a pinch of salt, garlic and vinegar. Whisk in the oil to taste. Set aside.

Wash the frisée and separate into bite-size pieces into a salad bowl. Slice the Belgian endive at an angle ¼" thick, and add to the bowl.

Cook the bacon until firm but not too crisp, drain on paper towels.

Pan-roast the venison to medium-rare, about 4 to 5 minutes, then let rest 5 minutes. Season to taste.

Cut or crush the walnuts into slightly smaller pieces. Cut the bacon into bite-size pieces and sprinkle on the salad with the walnuts. Toss with ¾ of the vinaigrette. Adjust seasonings to taste.

Divide the salad onto 8 serving plates. Slice the venison thinly and place it on and around the salad. Drizzle the remaining dressing over the top, as desired. Garnish with quail egg halves.

Trade Secret: Serve with a hearty sourdough French bread.

Serves 8
Preparation Time:
  45 Minutes

- 4 **shallots, minced**
  Salt
- 1 **garlic clove, lightly crushed**
- 3 **Tbsps. sherry vinegar**
- ¾ **cup walnut oil**
- 3 **small heads frisée (small, curly endive)**
- 4 **Belgian endive**
- ¼ **lb. bacon**
- 1 **lb. venison, tender cut, cut to 1" pieces**
  Salt and pepper to taste
- ¼ **cup walnut halves, roasted**
- 8 **quail eggs, hard-boiled, optional**

☆

Pan Roasted Rabbit with Mustard Sauce

Serves 8
Preparation Time:
  45 Minutes

  4 rabbits
  ¼ cup (½ stick) butter
    Salt and pepper to
    taste
  ¼ cup white wine
  ¼ cup port
  4 shallots, finely
    chopped
  1 cup heavy cream
  ¼ cup whole grain
    mustard
  1 tsp. hot Dijon mustard

Remove the legs and filets from the rabbits. Remove sinews from the filets. Bone the legs by first taking out the hip bone, then the kneecap. Cut around the thigh bone from each end to detach it and pull it out of the leg meat, so that the meat is intact. Do not open the leg from the side.

Pan roast the legs and filets separately in butter for about 5 minutes for the filets and 10 minutes for the legs. The legs are done when the centers start to turn opaque. Keep the rabbit in a warm oven for 5 minutes. Salt and pepper to taste.

Drain the excess fat from the rabbit pans and add the white wine, 2 Tbsps. port and the shallots. Reduce to 1 Tbsp. liquid and add the cream. Bring to a boil. Remove from heat and add both mustards and the remaining port. Salt and pepper to taste. If you reheat the sauce, do not bring it to a boil.

To serve, slice the filets on the bias and slice the legs crosswise. Place the rabbit on top of the sauce.

☆

Pear Almond Cream Tart

Pre-bake the pastry shell according to manufacturer's instructions.

Bring the water and 2 cups sugar to boil. Add the lemon juice to taste. The mixture should be tart.

Peel and core pears and place in the syrupy mixture. Bring to a boil, cover and simmer until the pears can be pierced with a knife. The pears should cool in the syrup and can be refrigerated in the syrup up to 7 days in a closed container.

Mix the dry ingredients, except the almonds, together in one bowl.

In a separate bowl combine the eggs, yolks, and ¼ cup milk. Pour the egg mixture into the dry ingredients and whip until light in color.

Scald the remaining milk in a saucepan over high heat. Pour half of the hot milk into the egg mixture. Mix well, then pour the egg mixture into the hot milk and return to medium heat. Stir constantly until the cream is smooth, thick and bubbling. Stir in the butter and vanilla. Transfer the pastry cream to a bowl and add the almonds. Fill the tart shell with the pastry cream to within ⅛″ from the top.

Slice the pear halves crosswise in ⅛″ slices to make 8 halves, sliced. Arrange the pears with the bottom of the pear towards the outside edge of tart and the tops at center, face down. Dot each pear with a pea-sized piece of butter and sprinkle with granulated sugar. Bake at 375° for 10 to 15 minutes or until bubbling and brown on top.

Trade Secret: This recipe can be made the day before and then assembled and baked the day of serving.

Serves 8
Preparation Time:
  1 Hour, 15 Minutes
Baking Time:
  15 Minutes

  1 **12″ round pastry shell**
  2 **cups water**
2⅔ **cups sugar**
    Juice of 2 lemons
  4 **pears**
  2 **Tbsps. cornstarch**
  ⅓ **cup flour**
  2 **eggs**
  3 **egg yolks**
  2 **cups milk**
  1 **Tbsp. butter**
  1 **tsp. vanilla**
  ½ **cup almonds, coarsely**
    chopped
    Butter and sugar for
    topping

THE SCOTTISH LION INN

AMERICAN-SCOTTISH CUISINE
Route 16, P.O. Box 1527
North Conway, New Hampshire
(603) 356-6381
Lunch Monday–Saturday 11:30AM–2PM
Brunch Sunday 10:30AM–2PM
Dinner Sunday–Friday 5:30PM–9PM
　　　　Saturday 5:30PM–9:30PM
AVERAGE DINNER FOR TWO: $50

S cottish pride pervades the Lion, with tartan trim abounding and kilted waitresses. Views of meadows and mountains, candlelit tables and lilting Scottish tunes set the festive, yet civilized spirit of the famous restaurant and pub.

Hot Scottish oatcakes, from an old family recipe, are served each evening with dinner. The celebrated Sunday brunch draws locals and tourists alike, and the pub offers over 55 genuine Scotches. Guests of the inn's seven comfortable, clan-named rooms are treated to a hearty, eye-opening breakfast, included in their room rates.

Chef/owner Michael Procopio's unique and varied menu includes Scallops Stuffed with Crabmeat, then baked in a Scottish Liqueur; Steak and Mushroom Pie; Highland Game Pie of Rabbit; Venison and Pheasant braised in Port, Chablis and Herbs; and a variety of imported ales.

THE SCOTTISH LION INN'S MENU FOR SIX

Tomato Cheddar Soup

Brunswick Stew

Kona Coffee Freeze

Tomato Cheddar Soup

I n a large saucepan, sauté the onion in butter until soft. Stir in the tomato purée, 2½ cups water, cheese and salt. Cook over medium heat, stirring constantly, until the cheese melts. Do not allow to boil. Remove from heat and cool for 10 minutes.

In a mixing bowl, combine the sour cream and 3 cups water. Slowly stir the cream mixture into the soup.

Serves 6
Preparation Time:
   25 Minutes

   1 medium onion, finely
      chopped
   ¼ cup butter (½ stick)
   1 can tomato purée
   5½ cups water
   1¼ cups cheddar cheese,
      shredded
   ½ tsp. salt
   1 cup sour cream

☆

Brunswick Stew

Serves 6
Preparation Time:
  30 Minutes
Cooking Time:
  45 Minutes

  1 **rabbit, 4 lbs., cut into**
    8 pieces each, well-
    rinsed and patted dry
 ½ **cup butter**
  1 **cup onions, chopped**
  1 **medium carrot,**
    ½″ **dice**
  1 **stalk celery,** ½″ **dice**
  2 **cups tomato, peeled,**
    seeded, chopped
  2 **cups lima beans**
 ¼ **tsp. cayenne pepper**
 ¼ **tsp. thyme**
  2 **cups chicken stock**
    Salt and pepper to
    taste

Dumplings, optional:
 ¼ **cup butter**
  1 **egg**
  1 **cup flour**
 ⅛ **tsp. salt**
  2 **Tbsps. milk, cold**

S auté the rabbit in butter until lightly browned. Remove the rabbit and sauté the onions, carrot and celery. Cook for 5 minutes or until onions are golden brown. Replace the rabbit and add the remaining ingredients. Simmer for 45 minutes. Season to taste.

To make the dumplings, beat together the butter and egg in a mixing bowl until creamy. Stir in the flour and salt. Slowly add the milk.

Form into small balls and cook in simmering water for 10 minutes. Do not let water boil when cooking the dumplings or they will become tough.

Just before serving, place the dumplings in the stew.

Kona Coffee Freeze

I n a mixing bowl combine the rum, coffee liqueur, macadamia nut liqueur, chocolate syrup, ice cream and Kona coffee.

Pour into 6 glasses over crushed ice. Garnish the top of each glass with whipped cream and macadamia nuts.

Serves 6
Preparation Time:
  5 Minutes

- ½ cup dark rum
- ½ cup Keoke coffee liqueur
- 6 Tbsps. macadamia nut liqueur
- ½ cup chocolate syrup
- 1 cup + 2 Tbsps. vanilla ice cream or frozen yogurt
- 1½ cups Kona coffee, fresh-brewed, cold
- Crushed ice to fill each glass
- Whipped cream, for topping
- Macadamia nuts for garnish

☆

CHRISTMAS FARM INN

Box CC, Route 16 B
Jackson, New Hampshire 03846
(800) HI ELVES (443-5837)
(603) 383-4313
ROOM RATES: $76–$110
AMENITIES: Thirty-eight rooms with private baths in one of several buildings, some with fireplace or jacuzzi, beamed ceilings, restaurant, children's play area, cocktail lounge, library, game rooms with large-screen TV, pool, putting green, sauna, volleyball. Cross-country skiing in winter. Near downhill skiing, sleigh rides, ice skating, hiking, canoeing and fishing.
DIRECTIONS: Take Route 16 north from Glen, exit on 16A into Jackson. Turn right onto 16B; the inn is on the right.

T he famous Christmas Farm Inn is not to be missed at any time of year. Rooms, suites, restaurant, reception hall/convention area and recreation rooms are divided among the village inn buildings of the Main Inn, the Salt Box, the Barn, the Log Cabin, the Sugar House and Deluxe Cottages. Choices range from cozy rooms for two, to romantic suites with jacuzzi, to cottages perfect for active families. The Main Inn and the Salt Box date from the late 18th century. The big, red barn hosts four deluxe suites upstairs and a sauna and 12-foot fireplace downstairs, as well as the reception hall.

For picturesque scenery, great skiing and a family getaway, the Christmas Farm is just right. Shop Jackson, ski Mt. Washington, or relax at the poolside cabana. As the Zeliff family owners say, "There is always something to do or not to do."

Grilled Quail Appetizer with Ham and Cucumber Salad

P lace the quail in a single layer in a shallow pan, cover with orange juice and marinate overnight.

Prepare the salad by combining the cucumbers, ham, carrot, mayonnaise, sage, pepper and garlic powder. Mix well.

Remove the quail from the orange juice and sprinkle each with a pinch of salt and 1 tsp. jerk seasoning, covering both sides well.

Grill over medium-high heat for 6 to 8 minutes until done.

Serve each quail with ½ cup of the ham and cucumber salad.

Serves 6
Preparation Time:
  25 Minutes
(note marinating time)

  6 **quail, semi-boneless**
  2 **cups orange juice**
  2 **medium cucumbers,**
    peeled, seeded, sliced
  1 **cup ham, diced**
  1 **carrot, grated**
 ½ **cup mayonnaise**
 ½ **tsp. sage**
    Pepper to taste
    Garlic powder to taste
 ⅛ **tsp. salt**
  2 **Tbsps. Caribbean jerk**
    seasoning

Veal Basilico

Serves 4
Preparation Time:
  35 Minutes

  4 **1-lb. veal cutlets,**
      ¼″ thick
      Salt and pepper to
      taste
  ¼ **cup flour**
  1 **to 2 Tbsps. olive oil**
  1 **Tbsp. garlic, chopped**
  ½ **lb. mushrooms, sliced**
  1 **medium onion, diced**
  ¾ **cup beef stock**
  1 **large tomato,**
      blanched, peeled,
      seeded, diced
      or ½ cup canned diced
      tomatoes, drained
  2 **Tbsps. fresh basil,**
      chopped

S eason the veal with salt and pepper. Dip each piece of veal into flour and shake off excess.

Add the oil to a hot sauté pan and add the veal one piece at a time. Do not overcrowd the pan. Turn each piece when lightly brown, after 1 to 2 minutes. Brown the other side. Remove from the pan and keep warm.

Add more oil to the pan if necessary and cook the garlic, mushrooms and onions. Sauté 2 to 3 minutes and add the stock. Reduce by half and add the tomato and basil. Simmer 1 to 2 minutes longer. Season to taste and serve the sauce over the veal.

Vegetable Stuffed Chicken

L ay out chicken breasts flat on a sheet pan. Divide each of the vegetable sticks among the chicken, placing them in the lobes where the bones were. Fold each breast around the vegetables. Coat each breast with a mixture of the bread crumbs and 2 Tbsps. Parmesan cheese.

Place the breasts at least ½" apart with the seam side down in a shallow baking dish. Bake at 400° until chicken is cooked and brown, about 15 to 20 minutes.

Heat cream and bouillon cube on high heat until reduced by half, about 8 to 10 minutes. Remove from heat and add remaining Parmesan. Stir well.

To serve, cut each breast into 4 or 5 slices and fan out slightly to view the vegetables. Spoon sauce over chicken.

Serves 6
Preparation Time:
   40 Minutes

   6 chicken breasts, 6-8 oz.
     each, skinless, boneless
  12 celery stalks, cut
     4"×¼"
   3 scallions, cut into
     4" sticks
   ¼ lb. snow peas, cut in
     thirds lengthwise
   1 medium red bell
     pepper, julienned
  1½ cups seasoned bread
     crumbs
   ¼ cup + 2 Tbsps.
     Parmesan cheese,
     grated
   2 cups heavy cream
   1 chicken bouillon cube

THE TAMWORTH INN

Main Street
Tamworth, New Hampshire 03886
(800) 933-3902
(603) 323-7721
ROOM RATES: $85–$160
AMENITIES: Ten rooms with private baths, 4 suites, pub, restaurant, full breakfast included, fireplaces in the living room, library and breakfast room, screened back porch, three acres bordered by the Swift River, fishing, barn, pool, gazebo, walking distance to cross-country ski trails and summer theater. Meeting facilities with computers, A/V equipment available. Pets allowed.
DIRECTIONS: Take Exit 23 from I-93 East. Take Route 104 for 12 miles to Route 3 North. Take Route 3 for 2 miles to Route 25 East. Take Route 25 18 miles to Route 113 West to Tamworth.

Each room in the 160-year-old Tamworth Inn is individually decorated with antiques and handmade quilts. The rooms have a homey feeling and are full of little comforts. Originally designed and built as an inn, it is roomy and well laid-out. The library features a fireplace, books, games, television and videos. Activities include summer theater, hiking, swimming, fishing, boating, bicycling, skiing, outlet shopping, antiquing and relaxing. The grounds cover 3 acres bordering the river, with on-site fishing. Across the street is a 40-acre thoroughbred pasture, leading to cross-country ski trails.

The chef is known for his Roast Duckling a L'Orange and the best Rack of Lamb within 100 miles. Breakfast specialties include Baked Eggs, Belgian "Wonderful" Waffles and fresh baked Rolls, Muffins and Breads.

Tortilla Soup

Sauté onions in a large saucepan in oil until transparent. Add the tomatoes and cook, stirring until the tomatoes are softened. Remove from heat and purée in a blender or food processor.

Return to the saucepan and add the remaining ingredients, except the tortilla strips and cheese. Simmer, stirring occasionally, about 30 minutes.

Add the tortilla strips and heat about 10 minutes.

Add the cheese and serve.

Serves 6
Preparation Time:
   20 Minutes
Cooking Time:
   40 Minutes

1 medium onion, chopped
4 Tbsps. vegetable oil
2 lbs. large tomatoes, chopped
6 cups chicken stock
1 Tbsp. cumin, ground
2 tsps. chile powder
1 Tbsp. garlic, chopped
1 can enchilada sauce
1 Tbsp. cilantro, chopped
2 tsps. green chiles, chopped
1 tsp. Worcestershire sauce
1 cup corn tortillas, cut in strips
1 cup cheddar cheese, shredded

WHITE GOOSE INN

Route 10, Box 17
Orford, New Hampshire 03777
(603) 353-4812
ROOM RATES: $75–$145
AMENITIES: Fourteen rooms, most with private bath, breakfast included. Area activities in-clude hiking, biking, camping, golfing, ice skating, skiing, sleigh rides. Near Dartmouth College.
DIRECTIONS: From I-91, take Exit 15 (Fairlee). Cross the bridge, then turn south on Route 10 and go one mile to the inn.

The White Goose Inn is an authentic colonial house, dating from 1833. The proud innkeepers of this establishment retain the traditional New England style. Each room has distinctive charm. Furnished with antiques, lace curtains and Oriental carpets, the inn demonstrates a commitment to warmth and quality.

The White Goose Inn is open year-round and offers guests a convenient location to the area's many attractions. Summer months bring hiking and biking over countless trails by rushing streams, through country villages and picturesque farmland, as well as fishing, camp-ing and golfing. Autumn at the White Goose places one in the midst of the finest foliage colors and near Dartmouth College activities. Winter guests are within minutes of the state's finest cross-country and downhill ski areas, as well as ice skating and sleigh rides.

French Toast

In a mixing bowl, combine the ice cream, egg and milk.

Cut the bread into thick slices, then dip into the milk mixture. Drip off any excess.

Heat the griddle with a little butter or margarine. Fry until golden brown on each side.

Dust with powdered sugar and serve with syrup.

Serves 4
Preparation Time:
  15 Minutes

1 cup vanilla ice cream,
  softened
2 large eggs
2 cups skim milk
1 loaf sweet Italian
  bread
  Butter for frying
  Powdered sugar
  Fruit or maple syrup

☆

MAINE:
Where The Sun
Rises First

Maine, the largest state in New England, measures 300 miles by 200 miles at its widest points. Yet the state is sparsely populated. In fact, of all the New England states, Maine alone offers vast, unspoiled open spaces.

Mention Maine to most people and the first thought they'll have is lobsters. That's because about 75 percent of the nation's lobsters are caught in Maine.

Former President George Bush brought more attention to the state because of his home in Kennebunkport. Another president — Franklin D. Roosevelt — also was associated with Maine because of his home at Campobello, even though the island of Campobello actually is in Canadian territory.

The state gained early economic importance because of its vast pine forests, which provided many a mast for early sailing ships. The decline of sailing vessels didn't diminish Maine's economy, however. The forests were vital to the lumber and paper-making industries. Other economic strength came from the harvesting of potatoes and in quarrying granite for construction. Today, tourism is the leading industry.

Originally part of Massachusetts, Maine became the 23rd state in 1820 as a result of the Missouri Compromise.

The state can be divided roughly into two distinctive parts — the busy and rugged coastal corridor and the relatively unspoiled interior that boasts countless lakes, rivers and streams, along with many miles of hiking trails.

One other claim to fame: the rising sun touches Maine before any other state.

Here are some highlights of a visit to Maine:

KENNEBUNKPORT — Best known as the site of President Bush's coastal home, the area consists of three communities: Kennebunk, Kennebunkport and Kennebunk Beach. Kennebunkport is one of the most popular vacation areas. The area is rich in historic houses; most of them are privately owned. An interesting spot is the Seashore Trolley Museum, which houses the world's largest collection of trolley cars. South of Kennebunkport lies Old York village, a "living history museum" that features the Old Gaol, an 18th century jail that now serves as a museum. Also south of Kennebunkport, look for the Wedding Cake House. Legend has it that the house was festooned with ornate woodwork because the builder, a sea captain, had to set sail in the middle of his wedding and he had the house completed as a

The first salmon of the year are sent to the President of the United States, even today.

An oceanside picnic in Maine.

Photos from the Bangor Historical Society.

consolation for his bride. North of Kennebunkport, you may want to stop at Biddeford Pool, considered one of the best bird-watching areas of the Atlantic coast.

PORTLAND — Once the state capital, Portland is Maine's largest city and its commercial center. Originally settled in 1633, the city has been destroyed four times: by Indians, by the French and Indians, by the British and by fire in 1866. Highlights include the Wadsworth-Longellow House, the boyhood home of poet Henry Wadsworth Longfellow and the first brick house in the city. The Portland Museum boasts works by Winslow Homer, Andrew Wyeth and Edward Hopper, as well as works by Monet, Degas, Picasso and Renoir. Nearby, you'll find Eagle Island, the home of Arctic explorer Admiral Robert E. Peary. The home, open for tours in the summer, houses many of Peary's belongings, including stuffed birds and other artifacts from the North Pole. North of Portland, on Sabbathday Lake, lies the last living Shaker community in the country. The community still has a few members who live in the Shaker tradition. The Shaker Museum includes a Meetinghouse circa 1794, a Spin House circa 1816 and a Ministry Shop circa 1839.

FREEPORT — Shoppers will want to make a pilgrimage to Freeport's most famous attraction, the L.L. Bean sporting goods store. The large store is open 24 hours a day, 7 days a week, all year long. The fascinating store, which has been in business for 75 years, features six parking lots and a trout pond inside the men's department. Over 100 factory outlet stores can be found nearby.

WISCASSET — This town claims to be the prettiest village in Maine. Once the busiest international port north of Boston, the town features beautiful homes and antique shops. The four-masted schooners *Hesper* and *Luther Little* lie decaying in the mud of Wiscasset. South of Wiscasset, visit Boothbay Harbor, where you can board boats for all sorts of cruises — from whale-watching to clambakes to visiting offshore islands, such as Cabbage Island and Monhegan Island. While in Boothbay Harbor, you may want to visit the Boothbay Theater Museum, which houses 200 years of theatrical memorabilia. The 142-foot fishing schooner *Sherman Zwicker* is moored at Boothbay Harbor and serves as a 19th-century fishing fleet museum.

ACADIA NATIONAL PARK — Maine's most popular tourist attraction, with 4 million visitors per year, Acadia National Park's 3,400 acres comprise about half of Mount Desert (pronounced "dessert") Island. The beautiful preserve contains many lakes, ponds and a clasic fjord. Attractions include Thunder Hole, where the tide crashes onto the shore, and the Robert Abbe Museum of Stone Age Antiquities. Cadillac Mountain, 1,530 feet high, is the highest point in America's Atlantic coast. People who drive or hike to the summit at daybreak are said to be the first people in the United States to see the sun.

Loggers break up a jam.

ARROWS

ECLECTIC CUISINE
P.O. Box 803, Berwick Road
Ogunquit, Maine
(207) 361-1100
Dinner 6PM–10PM
AVERAGE DINNER FOR TWO: $90

A true country restaurant, Arrows is set in an eighteenth-century farmhouse, one hour north of Boston. The dining room shows off the original plank floors, post and beam construction, and expansive glass walls overlooking a panorama of dense woods, trimmed lawns and Arrows' flower, herb and vegetable gardens. In addition to growing their own vegetables, chefs/owners Clark Frasier and Mark Gaier cure their own hams and fish, and bake all desserts and breads. Inside, the chefs present dramatic food and flower displays.

Nationally recognized and reviewed as a top dining establishment, Arrows' menu changes daily and reflects the diverse backgrounds of the chefs. Both worked with Jeremiah Tower at Stars Restaurant in San Francisco. Clark lived and studied in Beijing, China, and Mark was the executive chef of New England's Whistling Oyster.

Their menu may include Sautéed Foie Gras with Grilled Black Truffle Bread, Steamed Cockles with Sweet Chinese Sausage, Lettuce Cups with Maine Shrimp, Cucumber, Cilantro and Tamarind, Grilled Maine Scallops with Crab Wontons, Tenderloin of Beef Poached in Red Wine and Stock with Beet Purée, Marinated Venison with Warm Spinach, Dried Cherries and Tomato Compote, or desserts such as Pear Tartlette with Pear Sorbet and Caramel Sauce, and Apple Hazelnut Cake with Cinnamon Ice Cream.

ARROWS' MENU FOR FOUR

Szechuan Cabbage Salad

Lobster and Corn Fritters

Papaya Carrot Salad

Risotto with Tomatoes, Swiss Chard and Pancetta

Cucumber Compote

Szechuan Cabbage Salad

In a bowl, whisk together the chile paste, sesame oil, soy sauce, rice wine vinegar, ginger, garlic, salt, pepper and corn oil.

Toss the dressing with the cabbage in a large bowl and cover tightly.

Marinate the salad for 30 minutes to 1 hour. Serve with grilled or broiled meat or fish.

Serves 4
Preparation Time:
  10 Minutes
(note marinating time)

- 2 Tbsps. Chinese chile paste
- 2 Tbsps. dark sesame oil
- 2 tsps. soy sauce
- ¼ cup rice wine vinegar
- 2 tsps. fresh ginger, chopped
- 1 garlic clove, finely chopped
  Salt and pepper to taste
- 2 Tbsps. corn oil
- ½ head red cabbage, very finely sliced

Lobster and Corn Fritters

Serves 4
Preparation Time:
  20 Minutes

  ½ **cup flour**
  ¼ **tsp. salt**
  2 **tsps. baking powder**
  ½ **cup milk**
  1 **egg, lightly beaten**
    Meat of 1 whole
    lobster, cooked
  1 **cup corn kernels or**
    1 cup yam, raw,
    shredded
    Pepper to taste
    Oil for frying
    Fresh cilantro leaves
    for garnish

I n a mixing bowl combine the flour, salt and baking powder.
    In another bowl, stir together the milk and egg. Gradually add the milk mixture to the flour, just until mixture is smooth. Stir in the lobster and corn, or yam. Pepper to taste.

In a large skillet add enough oil to cover the bottom of the pan. Ladle the batter onto the hot oil to form 4 large fritters, about 3″ wide. Fry for 3 minutes on the first side, then about 2 minutes on the other side.

Garnish with cilantro and serve.

Papaya Carrot Salad

Peel both papayas and thinly slice them, removing the seeds.
　　Put the fruit in a bowl. Add the carrots, lime juice and vinegar. Sprinkle with sugar, then stir in chopped cilantro.

Serves 4
Preparation Time:
　15 Minutes

1　ripe papaya
1　green papaya
4　large carrots, shredded
　　Juice of 1 lime
1　Tbsp. rice wine vinegar
1　Tbsp. sugar
1　bunch fresh cilantro,
　　finely chopped

☆

Risotto with Tomatoes, Swiss Chard and Pancetta

Serves 4
Preparation Time:
 20 Minutes

 2 Tbsps. olive oil
 ½ large onion, chopped
 1 cup Arborio rice
 4 cups chicken stock, heated to boiling
 2 Tbsps. mixed herbs, chopped (tarragon, basil)
 ½ cup grated Asiago cheese
 12 slices pancetta or bacon
 4 Tbsps. butter
 2 heads Swiss chard, stems removed
 Salt and pepper to taste
 2 tomatoes, cored, sliced
 2 yellow tomatoes, cored, sliced

 In a heavy saucepan, heat the oil and sauté the onion over low heat for about 8 minutes until onion is soft but not brown. Stir in the rice and cook for 2 minutes.

 Add a ladle of chicken stock and stir constantly until the rice absorbs the stock. Add another ladle and continue stirring until it is absorbed. Add the herbs and continue stirring in the stock, one ladle at a time, until all has been used. Cook until the rice is creamy and tender. Stir in the cheese.

 While rice is cooking, cook the pancetta or bacon until crisp, then drain on a paper towel.

 Heat the butter, then add the Swiss chard. Salt and pepper to taste. Toss the chard in the butter until it is wilted.

 Divide the risotto among 4 plates, garnish with the crumbled pancetta and top with the Swiss chard. Arrange the tomatoes around the edge. Serve immediately.

Cucumber Compote

Halve the cucumbers lengthwise, then scoop out the seeds with a small spoon. Cut the cucumbers into cubes. Transfer them to a bowl and add the parsley, cilantro, onion, lemon juice, salt and pepper. Marinate 10 to 20 minutes before serving.

Serves 4
Preparation Time:
   15 Minutes

   2 cucumbers, peeled
   ½ bunch Italian parsley, finely chopped
   ½ bunch fresh cilantro, finely chopped
   ½ red onion, coarsely chopped
   Juice of 1 lemon
   Salt and pepper to taste

☆

BACK BAY GRILL

EUROPEAN/AMERICAN CUISINE
65 Portland Street
Portland, Maine
(207) 772-8833
Dinner Sunday–Thursday 5:30PM–9:30PM,
       Friday–Saturday 5:30PM–10PM
AVERAGE DINNER FOR TWO: $60

An elegant old brick building on a downtown corner is the setting of the Back Bay Grill. Outside, bright moldings and the gold-plated hanging sign give the first hint to diners of the ambiance they will find indoors. Original local art enhances the walls and menus; crisp white linens and single red roses adorn the tables. The staff pampers guests from the moment they enter. Owner and maitre d' Joel Freund calls an evening at his restaurant "Disneyland for grown-ups."

Head Chef Scott Anderson and his crew are impeccably trained and change the menu monthly to reflect local freshness. The wine list is extensive and the staff can help in selecting just the right one. Samples from the menu include Herbed Vermont Goat Cheese in Phyllo with Mushroom Vinaigrette, Crabmeat Spring Rolls, Sirloin with Red Pepper Vinaigrette, Atlantic Salmon Filet with a Lemon-Dill Crème Fraîche, Lemon Marinated Prawns, Rack of Lamb with Cranberries and Apple-Port Demi-Glace, Cornish Hen with a Hazelnut Flan, Lemon Chocolate Trifle with Raspberry Coulis, a Plum Crepe with Ginger Caramel Sauce and their signature Crème Brulée.

BACK BAY GRILL'S MENU FOR SIX

Grilled Portobellos and Fontina Gratinée with Onion Marmalade

Nut Crusted Trout with Grainy Mustard Cream and Matchstick Potatoes

Blackberry and Raspberry Gratin with Brown Sugar Crème Fraîche

Grilled Portobellos and Fontina Gratinée with Onion Marmalade

I n a mixing bowl, toss the onions with 6 Tbsps. olive oil, sea salt, peppercorns and vinegar. Spread the mixture in a shallow pan and roast in the oven at 450° for 20 minutes or until caramelized.

Coat the mushrooms with olive oil, sprinkle with salt and pepper. Grill the mushrooms 2 minutes on each side. Remove from the grill.

Stuff and mold the onion marmalade into the mushroom caps. Cover lightly with grated fontina and chopped parsley.

Place mushrooms under a hot broiler until the cheese turns brown and bubbly. Drizzle with olive oil and serve.

Serves 6
Preparation Time:
  30 Minutes
Pre-heat grill

12 medium portobello mushrooms, stems removed
 6 Tbsps. olive oil, + a little for coating
   Salt and pepper to taste
 6 red onions, thinly sliced
 4 Tbsps. balsamic vinegar
 1 tsp. peppercorns, cracked
 1 tsp. sea salt
12 oz. fontina cheese, grated
   Parsley, chopped

☆

Nut Crusted Trout with Grainy Mustard Cream and Matchstick Potatoes

Serves 6
Preparation Time:
  30 Minutes

  6 medium potatoes,
    cleaned, sliced
    Salt and pepper to
    taste
  2 Tbsps. canola oil, + oil
    for potatoes
  6 medium shallots,
    chopped
 ⅔ cup dry vermouth
  3 cups heavy cream
  3 Tbsps. grainy mustard
  2 cups almonds, peeled,
    slivered
  1 cup flour
  1 tsp. salt
 ½ tsp. white pepper
  6 trout
    Milk, for soaking fish

J ulienne the potato slices into matchsticks. Deep fry in canola oil until golden. Drain on paper towels and season with salt and pepper. Keep warm.

In a saucepan, combine the shallots and vermouth. Over low heat reduce to ⅓. Add the heavy cream and mustard and reduce to ⅓ or until thickened. Keep warm.

Roast the almonds in a hot oven. Place in a food processor and blend with the flour, salt and white pepper. Set aside.

Bone the trout entirely and separate the filets, halving the fish lengthwise, but leaving the skin on. Soak the filets briefly in milk. Dip the skin side only in the flour and nut mixture.

Heat a sauté pan and add 2 Tbsps. canola. Sauté the fish, skin side down, until golden. Place fish in a baking pan and finish in the oven, skin side up, at 400° for about 2 minutes.

To serve, place a serving of potatoes on each plate. Ladle a dollop of sauce beside the potatoes and criss-cross the filets over the sauce.

Trade Secret: Chef Scott Anderson recommends marinated asparagus tips with this dish.

Blackberry and Raspberry Gratin with Brown Sugar Crème Fraîche

Clean the berries and divide among 6 dessert dishes. Set aside.

Over medium heat in a saucepan mix ½ cup brown sugar and 3 Tbsps. water to dissolve the sugar. Remove from heat and add to the crème fraîche.

Mix the remaining brown sugar with white sugar in a mixing bowl.

Spoon the brown sugar crème fraîche over the berries to completely cover. Pour the sugar mixture over the crème fraîche.

Brown lightly for one minute under a hot broiler.

Serves 6
Preparation Time:
  15 Minutes

  1 pt. blackberries
  1 pt. raspberries
  ½ cup + ⅔ cup brown
     sugar
  3 Tbsps. water
3½ cups crème fraîche, or
     sour cream
  ⅔ cup sugar

☆

THE BELMONT

NEW ENGLAND CUISINE
6 Belmont
Camden, Maine
(207) 236-8053
Dinner 6PM–9PM
AVERAGE DINNER FOR TWO: $50

L ocated in Camden, Maine's oldest inn, the Belmont restaurant is rich in elegant details. From the fresh flowers, tasteful art and antiques to the stenciled floors, the Belmont adds its touch to the overall picturesque charm of the port town of Camden.

Chef and co-owner Jerry Clare is a self-taught and much-honored master of the kitchen, delighting visitors with such selections as Grilled Breast of Duck with an Oyster Mushroom Zinfandel Sauce, Three-Peppercorn Crusted Filet Mignon with a Brandy Demi-Glacé, and Grilled Venison Chops in a Juniper Berry Reduction. In addition, the Belmont features a vegetarian entrée nightly.

THE BELMONT'S MENU FOR SIX

Shrimp Soup

Lobster Pad Thai

Apple Cranberry Crostata

Shrimp Soup

Peel and devein the shrimp, reserving the shells.

In a large soup pot, place all of the shrimp shells, cover with cold water and add the carrots, cilantro stems, lemon grass stems and onion. Bring to a boil over low heat and simmer for 1 hour. Strain the shrimp stock into a clean pan, pressing down on the solids. Discard the solids and shells.

Combine the shrimp stock, lemon grass, chile paste, fish sauce, and Kaffer leaves. Bring to a boil. Lower heat and add the shrimp and mushrooms. Cook about 2 minutes.

Ladle into serving bowls. Garnish with red pepper flakes and cilantro. Serve lime wedge on the side.

Serves 6
Preparation Time:
 20 Minutes
Cooking Time:
 1 Hour

- 18 medium shrimp
- 2 carrots, sliced
- 2 Tbsps. fresh cilantro, chopped, stems reserved
- 2 Tbsps. lemon grass, minced, stems reserved
- 1 onion, quartered
- 1 Tbsp. chile paste
- 1 tsp. fish sauce
- 3 Kaffer lime leaves
- ½ cup shiitake mushrooms
- 2 Tbsps. red bell pepper, minced
- 1 lime, cut into 6 wedges
  Red pepper flakes for garnish
  Chopped Cilantro for garnish

★

Lobster Pad Thai

Serves 6
Preparation Time:
  40 Minutes

  3 lobsters, 1½ lbs. each
  ½ package rice-stick
    noodles
  ⅓ cup peanut oil
  2 Tbsps. fresh ginger,
    minced
  2 Tbsps. lemon grass
  1 bunch scallions,
    chopped, greens and
    whites separated
  1 tsp. chile paste
  3 Tbsps. shrimp paste
  3 Tbsps. pickled radish
  3 Tbsps. sugar
  1 Tbsp. lemon juice
  1 Tbsp. lime juice
  1 Tbsp. fish sauce
  1 egg, beaten with
    2 Tbsps. water
  3 Tbsps. cilantro,
    chopped
  1 cup peanuts, dry-
    roasted
  1 package mung bean
    sprouts
    Lemon wedges for
    garnish

Boil the lobster briefly. When cool enough to handle, remove the meat and refrigerate until needed.

Soak the noodles in lukewarm water for 15 minutes. Drain and set aside in a covered bowl.

Heat the peanut oil in a large non-stick frying pan. Working quickly, stirring or shaking the pan constantly, add the ginger, lemon grass and white scallions. Cook 1 minute, then add the lobster meat. Cook 4 minutes or until the meat is heated through. Add the chile paste, shrimp paste, radish and sugar. Cook 1 minute, then add the noodles, stirring them into the mixture. Add the lemon juice, lime juice and fish sauce; cook 1 minute. Add the beaten egg and green scallions; cook 1 minute.

Before serving, sprinkle with cilantro, peanuts and sprouts. Garnish with lemon wedges.

Trade Secret: Rice-stick noodles, chile paste, shrimp paste, pickled radish, lemon grass, and fish sauce can be purchased at Oriental food stores.

Apple Cranberry Crostata

I n the bowl of a food processor, combine the flour, ⅓ cup sugar and salt. Pulse. Add ⅓ cup butter and shortening and pulse until the mixture resembles cornmeal.

Transfer into a large mixing bowl and add the water. Shape the dough into a log and refrigerate for 1 hour.

Prepare the topping by combining the remaining flour and sugar with the cinnamon. Add ¼ cup butter. Set aside.

For the filling, combine the apple pieces and cranberries. Set aside.

To assemble, cut the dough into 8 equal portions. Working on a floured surface, roll each portion into a 6" disk about ¼" thick. Place ⅛ of the filling into the center of each. Gently raise the sides of the disks, draping them over the filling. Press down on the bottom edges.

Transfer each to a baking sheet and sprinkle the tops with the topping. Bake at 450° for about 15 minutes.

Serves 6
Preparation Time:
   15 Minutes
(note refrigeration time)
Cooking Time:
   15 Minutes

2¼ cups all-purpose flour
 ⅓ cup + ¼ cup sugar
 2 tsps. salt
 ⅓ cup + ¼ cup butter, unsalted, cut into small pieces
 ⅓ cup shortening
 2 to 3 Tbsps. ice water
 2 tsps. cinnamon
 4 large apples, peeled, sliced
 1 cup cranberries, washed

CAFÉ ALWAYS

NEW AMERICAN CUISINE
47 Middle Street
Portland, Maine
(207) 774-9399
Dinner Tuesday–Saturday 5PM–10PM
AVERAGE DINNER FOR TWO: $50

C afé Always is known for its eclectic menu and elegant atmosphere. The restaurant has been recognized nationally for its superb food and creative presentations. Chef and co-owner Cheryl Lewis, together with business partner Norine Kotts, change the menu daily, based on what is fresh in the market. In addition to the regular menu, they also offer a four-course prix-fixe tasting menu featuring the cuisine of a specific country or region. The interior of the 35-seat restaurant is decorated with a hand painted Victorian wallpaper mural by Portland artist Toni Wolf.

The menu is one of "mingling influences" rather than merely reproducing classic dishes of a specific cuisine. The owners' motto is, "No food rules."

At Café Always, Lewis is likely to offer rare appetizers like Grilled Asparagus Spears served with warm Maine goat cheese and balsamic vinaigrette. Entrées display her wide range and may include Grilled Chicken Breast served with Inner Beauty aioli and fresh Corn and Black Bean Salsa, Native Rabbit braised in a Rosemary Cream Sauce, or Grilled Five Spice Shrimp tossed with pasta and a Thai cilantro peanut sauce.

CAFÉ ALWAYS' MENU FOR FOUR

Oysters with Champagne and Pink Peppercorn Mignonette

Lobster with Thai Coconut Curry Sauce

Lemon Pudding Cake

Oysters with Champagne and Pink Peppercorn Mignonette

Peel the lemon with a vegetable peeler and chop the peel very fine. Measure 2 tsps. and place in a small saucepan. Add the peppercorns, champagne and sugar.

With a sharp knife, slice away all the white pith from the lemon. Section the lemon and dice each section into ¼″ cubes. Set aside.

Simmer the sauce over medium heat until reduced by half, 3 to 5 minutes. Remove from heat and add the diced lemon, shallots and vinegar.

To serve: Place oysters on the half shell on a bed of crushed ice and spoon a little sauce on each one.

Serves 4
Preparation Time:
  30 Minutes

  1 **large lemon**
1¼ **tsp. pink peppercorn**
  ½ **cup champagne or dry**
     sparkling wine
  1 **tsp. sugar**
  1 **tsp. shallots, minced**
 16 **oysters, rinsed and**
     opened

☆

Lobster with Thai Coconut Curry Sauce

Serves 4
Preparation Time:
  45 Minutes

  4 live lobsters, 1½ lbs.
    each
  2 garlic cloves, minced
  3 tsps. red Thai curry
    paste
1½ Tbsps. peanut oil
  1 red pepper, cut into
    ¼" strips
  1 yellow pepper, cut into
    ¼" strips
  1 can unsweetened
    coconut milk
  ¾ cup heavy cream
  2 tomatoes, cut into
    2" lengths
  ½ cup fresh basil leaves,
    packed
  ½ tsp. Thai fish sauce
  4 cups rice, cooked

Steam the lobsters in a large pot, by bringing 2" of cold water to a boil. Add the lobsters, cover and steam for 10 minutes. Remove from pot and allow to cool. Remove the meat from claws, knuckles and tail. Slice the tail meat in half lengthwise. Remove tomalley (the green liver) from cavity of lobster and reserve. This can be prepared a day ahead.

Prepare the sauce in a large saucepan by sautéing the garlic and curry in peanut oil over medium heat for 1 minute or until garlic is golden. Add the red peppers and sauté for 2 minutes. Add the coconut milk and reduce by half over high heat. Add the heavy cream and simmer for 3 to 4 minutes or until slightly thickened. Add the tomatoes, scallions, basil, fish sauce and lobster. Continue cooking for 1 minute or until heated through. Stir in reserved tomalley.

Serve with rice.

Lemon Pudding Cake

C ream the butter and sugar with an electric beater. Add the yolks one at a time, beating after each addition. Add the lemon juice, flour, cream, salt and nutmeg.

Beat the egg whites until soft peaks form and fold into the batter. Pour the mixture into a 6 cup baking dish or individual large ramekins.

Set into a larger baking dish filled with hot water half way up the sides. Bake until set, about 45 minutes.

Serve warm, room temperature, or cold.

Trade Secret: This dessert looks beautiful served in a pool of berry sauce or with a dollop of sweetened whipped cream.

Serves 6
Preparation Time:
  20 minutes
Baking Time:
  45 Minutes
Preheat oven to 350°F

  3 **Tbsps. butter**
  ¾ **cup sugar**
  4 **eggs, separated**
  ⅓ **cup lemon juice**
  3 **Tbsps. flour**
  1 **cup light cream**
  ⅛ **tsp. salt**
  ⅛ **tsp. nutmeg**

☆

THE CASTINE INN

REGIONAL MAINE CUISINE
Main Street
Castine, Maine
(207) 326-4365
Dinner 5:30PM–8:30PM
AVERAGE DINNER FOR TWO: $35

The Castine Inn's dining room is renowned for classic New England fare. Murals of the preserved Victorian seaside town, painted by co-owner Margaret Hodesh, span the walls of the room, and you can glimpse the harbor from the windows. The inn itself is spacious, warm and inviting.

Chef/owner Mark Hodesh offers dinner guests such starters as Duck Trap Smoked Trout with Cucumber Relish or Spinney Creek Oysters on the Half Shell. The main course immerses diners in true Maine flavors with Broiled Swordfish in Black Olive Sauce or Chicken and Leek Pot Pie, all complemented with sumptuous biscuits. Finish the experience with the perfect homemade dessert, Chocolate Torte with Coffee Custard Sauce or Tapioca Pudding with Apricot Sauce.

THE CASTINE INN'S MENU FOR FOUR

Baked Eggplant and Tomato Salad with Aioli

Crabmeat Cakes with Mustard Sauce

Blueberry Pie

Baked Eggplant and Tomato Salad with Aioli

Slice the eggplant into ½″ thick slices. Salt both sides and let stand in a colander for 45 minutes, to drain the bitterness. Rinse well and pat dry.

Combine ¼ cup olive oil, lemon juice, thyme and garlic. Toss the eggplant slices in the mixture.

Lightly brush a baking sheet with olive oil and place the slices on the sheet in a single layer. Cover tightly with aluminum foil and bake at 350° for 30 minutes or until tender.

Cool the slices on the baking sheet and remove with a spatula to a flat container. Slices can be layered with waxed paper. Pour any remaining olive oil mixture over the slices and refrigerate. Can be prepared one day in advance.

Blanch and peel the tomatoes. Slice into ½″ thick slices.

Combine the balsamic vinegar with ¾ cup olive oil and drizzle over the tomatoes.

To make the aioli, toss the garlic cloves lightly with ¼ cup olive oil. Place in a tightly covered baking dish and roast at 350° for 30 minutes or until the garlic is completely soft. Slide the cloves from their skins into a food processor and add the egg yolk, lemon juice and water. Process the mixture and gradually add ½ cup olive oil to the running food processor. Add water to thin to desired consistency.

Serve with 3 slices of tomato on a plate, topped with 3 slices of eggplant. Garnish with basil leaves, season with salt and pepper. Drizzle the top with the aioli.

Serves 4
Preparation Time:
 1 Hour
Baking Time:
 1 Hour

 1 **large eggplant, unpeeled**
   Salt and pepper to taste
1¾ **cups olive oil**
   Juice of 1 lemon
 1 **tsp. fresh thyme, minced**
 1 **tsp. garlic, minced**
 3 **tomatoes**
¼ **cup balsamic vinegar**
 6 **garlic cloves, unpeeled**
 1 **egg yolk**
 1 **tsp. lemon juice**
 1 **Tbsp. water**
16 **basil leaves**

☆

Crabmeat Cakes with Mustard Sauce

Serves 4
Preparation Time:
  1 Hour
Baking Time:
  10 Minutes

  ½ cup onion, finely
     chopped
  1 Tbsp. butter
2½ Tbsps. parsley leaves,
     minced
  3 eggs, beaten lightly
  1 Tbsp. hazelnuts,
     ground, toasted
1½ Tbsps. milk
1¾ cups dry bread crumbs
  1 lb. crabmeat, fresh
  ⅓ cup dry vermouth
1½ Tbsps. red wine
     vinegar
  1 shallot, minced
  2 black peppercorns
  ¾ cup white fish stock or
     bottled clam juice
  1 cup heavy cream
     Salt and white pepper
     to taste
  ½ cup Dijon mustard
  ⅓ cup sour cream
  2 Tbsps. unsalted butter,
     melted
     Parsley and lemon
     wedges as garnish

In a small skillet over medium-low heat, sauté the onion in the butter, stirring occasionally, until golden. In a large mixing bowl, combine the cooked onion, parsley, eggs, hazelnuts and milk. Stir in 1¼ cups bread crumbs and the crabmeat.

To make the mustard sauce, combine the vermouth, vinegar, shallots and peppercorns in a saucepan. Bring the mixture to a boil and reduce until almost all the liquid is evaporated. Add the stock and boil until the sauce is reduced by half. Add the heavy cream and boil until reduced by one third. Remove the saucepan from heat and whisk in mustard and sour cream. Season to taste with salt and white pepper.

Strain the sauce through a fine sieve into a bowl and keep it warm and covered. The mustard sauce can be refrigerated for up to a week. Whisk to restore separation.

Preheat oven to 450°. Form the crab mixture into cakes, using ⅓ cup for each cake. Sprinkle the cakes with ½ cup bread crumbs, transfer them to a baking sheet and bake in the middle of the oven for 8 minutes. Preheat the broiler. Brush the tops of the cakes with melted butter and broil 4 inches from the heat for 2 to 3 minutes until golden.

Serve 2 crabmeat cakes in a pool of sauce on each plate. Garnish with chopped parsley and lemon wedges.

Blueberry Pie

In a saucepan, mix the cornstarch, salt, sugar, lemon zest, cinnamon, 1 cup blueberries and water. Cook, stirring constantly, over medium heat until the cornstarch is cooked and the mixture turns clear and thick.

Add the butter and remaining 3 cups blueberries. Remove from heat.

Pour the blueberry mixture into the pie shell. Chill.

Serve with whipped cream.

Serves 8
Preparation Time:
  15 Minutes

3 Tbsps. cornstarch
1/8 tsp. salt
1 cup sugar
  Zest of 1/2 lemon
1/2 tsp. cinnamon
4 cups blueberries
1 cup water
1 Tbsp. butter
1 pie shell, 9", pre-baked
  Whipped cream

JONATHAN'S

NEW ENGLAND CUISINE
Main Street, PO Box 315
Blue Hill, Maine
(207) 374-5226
Dinner Monday–Sunday 5PM–11PM
AVERAGE DINNER FOR TWO: $40

T his popular restaurant, known for its upscale cuisine, features an upstairs and a downstairs dining room. The downstairs room is older and sports captains' chairs, local art and blue linens. Upstairs, the warmth of wood envelops diners, from the post-and-beam construction to the elegant high-backed chairs. Candles in hurricane globes add to the ambiance. This restaurant boasts Maine's largest wine selection, with over 250 varieties from French and California vineyards.

Chef/owner Jonathan Chase, along with his sister Sarah Leah Chase, has authored the regional cookbook *Saltwater Seasonings, Good Food from Coastal Maine*. Jonathan has developed a loyal following of customers drawn to his warm hospitality and creative cookery.

The menu features a host of taste treats such as Lobster Ravioli with Smoked Shrimp, Peppercorn Duck, Local Mussels Steamed with Wine and Herbs, Ginger and Lime Marinated Yellowfin Tuna, and Pub-Style Black Angus Sirloin with Ale-Braised Onions.

JONATHAN'S MENU FOR SIX

Warm Salad with Smoked Mussels and Chèvre

Drunken Rabbit with Maple Barbecue Sauce

Southern Comfort Raisin Bread Pudding

Warm Salad with Smoked Mussels and Chèvre

F or the dressing, combine 1 cup olive oil, vinegar, sherry, garlic, shallot and thyme in a saucepan. Over medium heat, bring the mixture to a boil. Reduce to low heat and add the mussels. Simmer at least 5 minutes to get the smoky flavor from the mussels.

Assemble the greens on separate plates and sprinkle with pine nuts.

Cut the Chèvre into 6 equal pieces and place on an oiled baking sheet. Drizzle the remaining oil over the top of the cheese. Place the cheese in the oven at 350° and bake until just warm and beginning to melt, 1 to 2 minutes. Remove the cheese from the oven and place 1 piece in the middle of each bed of greens.

With a slotted spoon, remove the mussels from the dressing and divide them among the plates.

Whisk the dressing and distribute it over each salad until the heat begins to wilt the greens.

Top each salad with sprouts and pepper to taste.

Serves 6
Preparation Time:
15 Minutes

1⅛ cups olive oil
½ cup red wine vinegar
¼ cup dry sherry
1 large garlic clove, minced
1 shallot, minced
¼ tsp. dried thyme
½ lb. smoked mussels
½ lb. fresh greens
¼ cup pine nuts, toasted
½ lb. Chèvre
  Sprouts for garnish
  Pepper to taste

Drunken Rabbit
with Maple Barbecue Sauce

Serves 6
Preparation Time:
  15 Minutes
(note marinating time)
Cooking Time:
  2 Hours

  2 **rabbits, 2 lbs, each,
    cleaned, cut into
    serving pieces**
  4 **garlic cloves, coarsely
    chopped**
  2 **Tbsps. dried thyme**
  2 **Tbsps. dried rosemary**
  2 **tsps. salt**
  2 **tsps. dried mustard**
  ½ **cup olive oil**
  ½ **cup apple cider vinegar**
  2 **bottles of ale, 12 oz.
    each**
  3 **cups maple barbecue
    sauce**
  1 **large onion, peeled,
    halved, thinly sliced
    Salt and pepper to
    taste**

One day before planning to scrve the rabbit, toss the rabbit meat with garlic, thyme, rosemary, salt and mustard. Let stand 2 to 3 hours in the refrigerator.

Combine the olive oil, vinegar and ale. Pour over the rabbit and let marinate in the refrigerator overnight. Turn the pieces occasionally.

The next day, drain the rabbit pieces from the marinade. Reserve marinade. Arrange the pieces in a single layer in a large roasting pan.

Place the reserved marinade in a saucepan, bring to a boil on high heat, and cook until reduced by ⅓, 12 to 15 minutes. Add the barbecue sauce, salt, pepper, and onion and return to a low boil. Pour the sauce evenly over the rabbit in the roasting pan.

Cover roasting pan tightly with aluminum foil and bake at 350° until the rabbit is tender, about 1 to 1¼ hours. Serve immediately.

☆

Southern Comfort Raisin Bread Pudding

Place the raisins in Southern Comfort to soak. Bring the milk to a boil. Remove from heat and add the cream.

Whisk the eggs, yolks, sugar and vanilla together. Add this to the milk/cream mixture.

Butter the bread on both sides. Sprinkle half the raisins over the bottom of a 9"×13" glass baking dish. Uniformly place the bread in rows, with pieces overlapping, to fill the pan. Pour the Southern Comfort into the egg/milk mixture. Pour this over the bread in the baking dish. Gently press down on the bread to momentarily submerge it so that it soaks up as much liquid as possible, to prevent burning when baking. Sprinkle the remaining raisins over the top of the pudding.

Place the pudding in a larger pan with enough water to come halfway up the sides of the baking dish. Bake at 350° for about 1 hour until the custard is just set.

Cool to room temperature and dust with powdered sugar.

Serves 8
Preparation Time:
  15 Minutes
Cooking Time:
  1 Hour

  1 cup raisins
  ⅓ cup Southern Comfort
  5 cups milk
  1 cup whipping cream
  7 eggs
  4 egg yolks
  1½ cups sugar
  1½ tsps. vanilla extract
  1½ loaves French bread, preferably day-old, cut diagonally into 40 slices
  1 cup (2 sticks) butter, unsalted, room temperature
  2 Tbsps. powdered sugar

☆

THE BELMONT

6 Belmont
Camden, Maine 04843
(207) 236-8053
ROOM RATES: $75–$145
AMENITIES: Six rooms and suites, all with private bath. Gazebo and wrap-around porch, full-service restaurant. Near hiking, watersports and antique shops of Camden.
DIRECTIONS: Turn east off U.S. 1 onto Belmont Avenue at the flashing light at the southern end of town. Follow Belmont Avenue for 2 blocks.

The Belmont is a quiet haven in the midst of Camden. The inn has 99 windows, allowing light to flood the immaculate, charming rooms and fresh flowers everywhere. The building is a beautifully restored Edwardian, Camden's oldest inn.

Celebrated chef and co-owner Jerry Clare has made the restaurant one of the finest and offers imaginative menus with skillfully blended local food, such as Grilled Marinated Quail, Grilled Breast of Duck with Oyster Mushroom Zinfandel Sauce, Three-Peppercorn Crusted Filet Mignon with Brandy Demi-Glace, and Grilled Venison Chop in a Juniper Berry Sauce. The Belmont also always features a daily vegetarian entrée.

Stir-Fry Mussels

I n a large sauté pan, heat oil on high heat. Add shrimp paste, chile paste, hoisin sauce, ginger, lemon grass, and sugar and cook 1 minute, stirring to blend all ingredients.

Add the mussels all at once, shaking the pan so the mussels are coated. Add the fish sauce and lime juice. Cover the pan and cook for 5 minutes until all the shells have opened. Pour onto a large platter and garnish with red pepper, scallions and cilantro.

Serves 6
Preparation Time:
  10 Minutes

  3 **Tbsps. oil**
  2 **Tbsps. shrimp paste**
  2 **Tbsps. chile paste**
  2 **Tbsps. hoisin sauce**
  2 **Tbsps. fresh ginger,**
    chopped
  2 **Tbsps. lemon grass,**
    chopped
  1 **Tbsp. sugar**
36 **mussels, rinsed,**
    debearded
  1 **Tbsp. fish sauce**
    Juice of 1 lime
  2 **Tbsps. red bell pepper,**
    minced
  1 **cup scallions, sliced**
  2 **Tbsps. fresh cilantro,**
    chopped

☆

THE CASTINE INN

Main Street
Castine, Maine 04421
(207) 326-4365
ROOM RATES: $75–$140
AMENITIES: Twenty rooms, all with private baths. Complimentary full breakfast. Full-service dining room and pub. Piazza with tables, chairs and view of harbor.
DIRECTIONS: I-95 to Route 1. Turn south on Hwy. 175, continue as 175 becomes Hwy. 166. Take 166 or 166A to Castine.

T he Castine Inn is a large, century-old Victorian inn in the heart of Castine, a beautiful coastal Maine town. Owners Mark Hodesh and Margaret Parker welcome guests on the sprawling piazza with a magnificent view of Castine's harbor and the gardens.

The dining room, decorated with whimsical murals, is open to the public for breakfast and dinner. The menu features traditional New England fare. Specialties include Maine Lobster, Crabmeat Cakes with Mustard Sauce, Chicken and Leek Pot Pies and outrageous Buttermilk Biscuits.

Buttermilk Biscuits

Sift the dry ingredients together in a mixing bowl. Cut in the shortening with a pastry cutter or by hand. In a separate bowl, whisk together the buttermilk, 2 eggs and water.

Make a well in the dry ingredients and add the liquid. Work lightly by hand until dry ingredients are just moist.

Turn out on a floured surface and pat down gently to 1½″ thick. Cut with a 2″ biscuit cutter and place on a baking pan.

Lightly beat the remaining egg, and brush the tops of the biscuits.

Bake at 400° for about 15 minutes or until golden brown.

Serves 4
Preparation Time:
  10 Minutes
Baking Time:
  15 Minutes

4 cups cake flour
1½ tsps. salt
¼ cup sugar
¼ tsp. nutmeg
2½ Tbsps. baking powder
1 cup vegetable
  shortening
1 cup buttermilk
3 eggs
⅓ cup water

☆

HARTSTONE INN

41 Elm Street
Camden, Maine 04843
800-788-4823
(207) 326-4365
ROOM RATES: $60–$120
AMENITIES: Eight rooms, all with private baths, two with fireplaces. Reading parlor with fireplace, as well as TV/game common room. Hearty New England breakfast included. Full service restaurant for dinner.
DIRECTIONS: Take I-95 north to Brunswick, then Coastal Route 1 north to Camden. Route 1 becomes Elm St. when it enters Camden. The Hartstone Inn, at 41 Elm St., is on the left as you enter the business district.

T he Hartstone Inn is a federal house built in 1835, with the third floor and Victorian adornments added in 1900. The rooms are bright and airy, decorated in antiques and furniture selected for comfort. The front parlor and dining rooms have fireplaces which lend a cozy feeling on crisp nights. The library has a wide selection of books on Maine and sailing as well as television and games. A new granite patio behind the inn is fenced for privacy and is a quiet place for iced tea and conversation.

Located in the village's business district, the inn offers direct access to fine shops, galleries and restaurants.

The harbor's windjammer fleet and many classic sailing yachts provide a daily parade of tall ships. The Camden Opera House, Camden Hills State Park and Lake Megunticook are all within a short walk or drive. Winter skiing is available at Camden Snow Bowl, and autumn foliage is spectacular.

The Hartstone offers a four-course, $50 prix fixe dinner for inn guests by reservation.

German Coffeecake

Mix flour, cinnamon, salt, brown sugar, sugar and vegetable oil. Set aside ¾ cup of mixture for topping.

Add baking soda and buttermilk to mixture. Mix well, then add baking powder and egg. Mix well again and pour into two greased and floured 8" cake pans. Sprinkle on topping and walnuts.

Bake at 350° for 35 or 40 minutes.

Serves 8
Preparation Time:
  15 Minutes
Baking Time:
  40 Minutes

2½ cups flour
  1 tsp. cinnamon
  ½ tsp. salt
  1 cup brown sugar
  1 cup sugar
  ¾ cup vegetable oil
  1 tsp. baking soda
  1 cup buttermilk
  1 tsp. baking powder
  1 egg, beaten
  ½ cup walnuts, chopped

Hartstone Baked Eggs

Serves 6
Preparation Time:
  10 Minutes
Baking Time:
  20 Minutes

  1 **cup ham, finely**
     chopped
  1 **cup cheese of choice,**
     finely chopped
  2 **Tbsps. chives, chopped**
  2 **Tbsps. half and half**
  6 **large eggs**
     Salt and white pepper
     to taste

Mix together the ham, cheese and chives.
Place 2 Tbsps. of the mixture in the bottom of half-cup ramekins. Add 1 tsp. half and half. Break egg over the mixture. Salt and pepper to taste.

Place ramekins in a 9″×13″ baking pan. Pour boiling water around the ramekins to a depth of ½″.

Bake for 20 minutes at 400° or until the white is done and yolk is soft.

Poached Pears with Raspberry Sauce

Peel the pears, but leave the stem intact. Cut a small slice off the bottom of each pear to make it sit flat.

Place the pears in a saucepan and add the water and lemon juice. Bring to a boil, then cover, lower heat and simmer 10 minutes or until a fork easily pierces the flesh. Drain liquid.

Cover pears and chill several hours or overnight.

To prepare the sauce, combine the raspberries, orange juice, liqueur and sugar in a food processor and blend thoroughly. Strain through a fine sieve to remove seeds. Adjust seasonings to taste.

To serve, place the chilled pears on a dessert plate and ladle the sauce over the fruit.

Serves 6
Preparation Time:
30 Minutes
(note refrigeration time)

- 6 pears, firm
- 4 cups water
  Juice of one lemon
- 2 cups fresh, or 10 oz. frozen, raspberries
- ½ cups orange juice
- 2 Tbsps. creme de cassis
- ⅓ cup sifted powdered sugar

Mashed Potatoes with Scallions

Serves 6
Preparation Time:
  30 Minutes
Baking Time:
  15 Minutes

  3 lbs. potatoes
  ⅔ cup sour cream
  ¼ cup butter
  4 scallions, chopped

Peel the potatoes and cut into ½" slices. Cover with water and bring to a boil. Lower heat and cook until tender, about 10 minutes. Drain and put through a food mill.

With an electric mixer, beat into the potatoes the sour cream, butter and scallions. Spoon into a 1½ qt. baking dish.

Bake at 400° for 15 minutes.

Salmon with Green Peppercorns

Brush the top of the fish with butter or oil and place skin side down on a baking dish. Broil 3″ from the flame for about 5 minutes.

Crush the peppercorns and sprinkle over the fish. Cook another few minutes (total of 10 minutes for each inch of thickness).

While the fish is cooking, reduce the lemon juice in a small pan by half. Add the butter and keep moving the pan while the butter melts. This should be done over a very low heat so the sauce does not separate.

When the fish is done, slip a spatula between the flesh and the skin. Lift the fish leaving the skin behind on the pan.

Spoon the sauce over the fish and serve immediately.

Serves 2
Preparation Time:
  20 Minutes

  4 salmon filets
    Oil
  3 Tbsps. peppercorns
  3 Tbsps. lemon juice
  8 Tbsps. (1 stick) butter

☆

Mail Order Sources

If you are unable to locate some of the specialty food products used in *New England's Cooking Secrets*, you can order them from the mail order sources listed below. These items are delivered by UPS, fully insured and at reasonable shipping costs.

CHEESE

Crowley Cheese
Healdsville Road
Healdsville, VT 05758
(802) 259-2340
Smoked, mild, medium and sharp cheeses, plus spiced cheeses such as garlic, sage and hot pepper.

Ideal Cheese
1205 Second Ave.
New York, NY 10021
(212) 688-7579
Imported Italian cheeses.

Mozzarella Company
2944 Elm St.
Dallas, TX 75226
(800) 798-2654
(214) 741-4072
(214) 741-4076 fax
Goat cheese, mascarpone, mozzarella, pecorino, ricotta and other cheeses.

Tillamook County Creamery Association
P.O. Box 313
Tillamook, OR 97141
(503) 842-4481
(800) 542-7290
Over 30 types of cheeses, black wax cheese, and a hot jalapeño cheese.

CHOCOLATES AND CANDY

The Brigittine Monks Gourmet Confections
23300 Walker Lane
Amity, OR 97101
(503) 835-8080
(503) 835-9662 fax
Popular items are chocolate with nuts and pecan pralines.

Festive Foods
9420 Arroyo Lane
Colorado Springs, CO 80908
(719) 495-2339
Spices and herbs, teas, oils, vinegars, chocolate and baking ingredients.

COFFEE AND TEA

Brown & Jenkins Trading Co.
P.O. Box 2306
South Burlington, VT
   05407-2306
(802)862-2395
(800) 456-JAVA
Water-decaffeinated coffees featuring over 30 blends such as Brown & Jenkins Special blend, Vermont Breakfast blend and Hawaiian Kona, in addition to 15 different flavors of teas.

Stash Tea Co.
P.O. Box 90
Portland, OR 97207
(503) 684-7944
(800) 826-4218
Earl Grey, herbal teas like peppermint, ruby mint, orange spice and licorice flavors.

DRIED BEANS AND PEAS

Baer's Best
154 Green Street
Reading, MA 01867
(617) 944-8719
Bulk or 1-pound packages of over 30 different varieties of beans, common to exotic. No peas.

Corti Brothers
5801 Folsom Blvd.
Sacramento, CA 95819
(916) 736-3800
Special gourmet items such as: imported extra-virgin olive oils, wines, exotic beans, egg pasta.

Dean & Deluca
560 Broadway
New York, NY 10012
(800) 221-7714
(212) 431-1691
Dried beans, salted capers, polenta, Arborio rice, dried mushrooms, dried tomatoes, Parmesan and reggiano cheeses, kitchen and baking equipment.

DRIED MUSHROOMS

Dean & Deluca
560 Broadway
New York, NY 10012
(800) 221-7714
(212) 431-1691
Dried beans, salted capers, polenta, Arborio rice, dried mushrooms, dried tomatoes, Parmesan and reggiano cheeses, kitchen and baking equipment.

G.B. Ratto & Co.
821 Washington St.
Oakland, CA 94607
(800) 325-3483
(510) 836-2250 fax
Imported pasta, dried beans, amaretti cookies, semolina flour, dried mushrooms, dried tomatoes, Parmesan and reggiano cheeses.

Gold Mine Natural Food Co.
1947 30th St.
San Diego, CA 92102-1105
(800) 475-3663
Organic foods, dried foods, whole grain rice, Asian dried mushrooms, condiments, sweeteners, spices.

FISH, CAVIAR AND SEAFOOD

Nelson Crab
Box 520
Tokeland, WA 98590
(206) 267-2911
(800) 262-0069
Fresh seafood as well as canned specialties like salmon, shrimp and tuna.

Legal Sea Foods
33 Everett Street
Boston, MA 02134
(617) 254-7000

(800) 343-5804
Live lobsters, fresh filets and seafood steaks, clam chowder, little neck steamer clams, shrimp, smoked Scottish salmon and Beluga caviar.

FLOURS AND GRAINS

Dean & Deluca
Dried beans, salted capers, polenta, Arborio rice, dried mushrooms, dried tomatoes, Parmesan and reggiano cheeses, kitchen and baking equipment.
See Dried Beans and Peas.

G.B. Ratto & Co.
821 Washington Street
Oakland, CA 94607
Flours, rice, bulgar wheat, couscous, oils, and sun-dried tomatoes.
See Dried Mushrooms.

Gold Mine Natural Food Co.
Organic foods, dried foods, whole grain rice, Asian dried mushrooms, condiments, sweeteners, spices.
See Dried Mushrooms.

King Arthur Flour Baker's Catalogue
P.O. Box 876
Norwich, VT 05055
(800) 827-6836
Semolina flour, all types of flours, wheat berries, kitchen and baking equipment.

The Vermont Country Store
P.O. Box 3000
Manchester Center, VT 05255-3000
(802) 362-2400 credit card orders
(802) 362-4647 customer service

Orders are taken 24 hours a day. Many different varieties: whole wheat, sweet-cracked, stone-ground rye, buckwheat, cornmeal and many more. They also sell a variety of items which are made in Vermont.

FRUIT & VEGETABLES

Diamond Organics
Freedom, CA 95019
(800) 922-2396
Free catalog available.
Fresh, organically grown fruits & vegetables, specialty greens, roots, sprouts, exotic fruits, citrus, wheat grass.

Giant Artichoke
11241 Merritt St.
Castroville, CA 95012
(408) 633-2778
Fresh baby artichokes.

Lee Anderson's Covalda Date Company
51-392 Harrison Street (Old Highway 86)
P.O. Box 908
Coachella, CA 92236-0908
(619) 398-3441
Organic dates, raw date sugar and other date products. Also dried fruits, nuts and seeds.

Northwest Select
14724 184th St. NE
Arlington, WA 98223
(800) 852-7132
(206) 435-8577
Fresh baby artichokes.

Timber Crest Farms
4791 Dry Creek Road
Healdsburg, CA 95448
(707) 433-8251

Domestic dried tomatoes and other unsulfured dried fruits and nuts.

HONEY

Howard's Happy Honeybees
4828 Morro Drive
Bakersfield, CA 93307
(805) 366-4962
Unfiltered flavored honeys, such as orange blossom and sage honeys in addition to honey candy.

KITCHEN AND BAKING EQUIPMENT

A Cook's Wares
211 37th St.
Beaver Falls, PA 15010-2103
(412) 846-9490

Dean & Deluca
560 Broadway
New York, NY 10012
(800) 221-7714
(212) 431-1691
Dried beans, salted capers, polenta, Arborio rice, dried mushrooms, dried tomatoes, Parmesan and reggiano cheeses, kitchen and baking equipment.

La Cuisine
323 Cameron St.
Alexandria, VA 22314
(800) 521-1176

The Chef's Catalog
3215 Commercial Ave.
Northbrook, IL 60062-1900
(800) 338-3232
(708) 480-8929

Williams-Sonoma
Mail Order Dept.
P.O. Box 7456
San Francisco, CA 94120-7456

(800) 541-2233 credit card orders
(800) 541-1262 customer service
Vinegars, oils, foods and kitchen-ware.

MEATS AND POULTRY

New Braunfels Smokehouse
P.O. Box 311159
New Braunfels, TX 78131-1159
(512) 625-7316
(800) 537-6932
A family owned business since 1945, selling quality hickory smoked meats, poultry, and fish. They also sell lean summer sausages, bacon, and beef jerky.

Omaha Steaks International
P.O. Box 3300
Omaha, NE 68103
(800)228-9055
Corn-fed Midwestern beef, filet mignon and boneless strips of sirloin.

Gerhard's Napa Valley Sausages
901 Enterprise Way
Napa, CA 94558
(707) 252-4116
Specializing in more than 26 types of fresh and smoked sausages: chicken apple, east Indian, turkey/chicken, Syrian lamb, kielbasa, Italian, Bavarian beerwurst, Cajun, duck with roasted almonds and much more. They do not use cereal fillers, MSG or artificial flavors.

Deer Valley Farm
R.D. #1
Guilford, NY 13780
(607) 764-8556

Organically raised chicken, beef and veal. These meats are very low in fat and high in flavor.

NUTS

Gourmet Nut Center
1430 Railroad Avenue
Orland, CA 95963
(916) 865-5511
Almonds, pistachios and cashews.

Koinonia Partners
1324 Hwy 49 South
Americus, GA 31709
(912) 924-0391
Shelled/unshelled, flavored pecans and peanuts in addition to chocolates and different varieties of fruitcakes.

PASTA

Corti Brothers
Special gourmet items such as: imported extra-virgin olive oils, wines, exotic beans, egg pasta.
See Dried Beans and Peas

G.B. Ratto & Co.
Imported pasta, dried beans, amaretti cookies, semolina flour, dried mushrooms, dried tomatoes, Parmesan and reggiano cheeses.
See Dried Mushrooms

Morisi's Pasta
John Morisi & Sons, Inc.
647 Fifth Avenue
Brooklyn, NY 11215
(718) 499-0146
(800) 253-6044
Over 250 varieties available from this 50-year old, family-owned gourmet pasta business.

PASTRY AND BAKED GOODS

Cafe Beaujolais Bakery
P.O. Box 730
Mendocino, CA 95460
(707) 937-0443
Panfortes, almond and hazelnut pastries as well as fruit cakes, jam, chocolate and home-made cashew granola.

SAFFRON

Vanilla Saffron Imports, Inc.
949 Valencia Street
San Francisco, CA 94110
(415) 648-8990
(415) 648-2240 fax
Saffron, vanilla beans and pure vanilla extract, dried mushrooms as well as herbs.

SEEDS FOR GROWING HERBS AND VEGETABLES

Herb Gathering, Inc.
5742 Kenwood Ave.
Kansas City, MO 64110
(816) 523-2653
Seeds for growing herbs, fresh-cut herbs.

Shepherd's Garden Seeds
6116 Highway 9
Felton, CA 95018
(408) 335-6910
Excellent selection of vegetable and herb seeds with growing instructions.

The Cook's Garden
P.O. Box 535
Londonderry, VT 05148
(802) 824-3400

Organically grown, reasonably priced vegetable, herb and flower seeds. Illustrated catalog has growing tips and recipes.

Vermont Bean Seed Company
Garden Lane
Fair Haven VT 05743
(802) 273-3400
Selling over 60 different varieties of beans, peas, corn, tomato and flower seeds.

W. Atlee Burpee & Co.
Warminster, PA 18974
(800) 888-1447
Well-known, reliable, full-color seed catalog.

Well-Sweep Herb Farm
317 Mount Bethal Rd.
Port Murray, NJ 07865
(908) 852-5390
Seeds for growing herbs, fresh herb plants.

SPECIALTY FOODS AND FOOD GIFTS

China Moon Catalogue
639 Post St.
San Francisco, CA 94109
(415) 771-MOON (6666)
(415) 775-1409 fax
Chinese oils, peppers, teas, salts, beans, candied ginger, kitchen supplies, cookbooks.

Corti Brothers
Special gourmet items such as: imported extra-virgin olive oils, wines, exotic beans, egg pasta.
See Dried Beans and Peas

Festive Foods
Spices and herbs, teas, oils, vinegars, chocolate and baking ingredients.
See Chocolates and Candy

G.B. Ratto & Co.
Imported pasta, dried beans, amaretti cookies, semolina flour, dried mushrooms, dried tomatoes, Parmesan and reggiano cheeses.
See Dried Mushrooms

Gazin's Inc.
P.O. Box 19221
New Orleans, LA 70179
(504) 482-0302
Specializing in Cajun, Creole and New Orleans foods.

Gold Mine Natural Food Co.
Organic foods, dried foods, whole grain rice, Asian dried mushrooms, condiments, sweeteners, spices.
See Dried Mushrooms

Knott's Berry Farm
8039 Beach Boulevard
Buena Park, CA 90620
(800) 877-6887
(714) 827-1776
Eleven types of jams and preserves, nine of which are non-sugar.

Kozlowski Farms
5566 Gravenstein Highway
Forestville, CA 95436
(707) 887-1587
(800) 473-2767
Jams, jellies, barbecue and steak sauces, conserves, honeys, salsas, chutneys and mustards. Some products are non-sugared, others are in the organic line. You can customize your order from 65 different products.

Williams-Sonoma
Vinegars, oils, foods and kitchen-ware.
See Kitchen and Baking Equip.

SPICES AND HERBS

Apple Pie Farm, Inc.
(The Herb Patch)
Union Hill Rd. #5
Malvern, PA 19355
(215)933-4215
A wide variety of fresh-cut herbs.

Festive Foods
Spices and herbs, teas, oils, vinegars, chocolate and baking ingredients.
See Chocolates and Candy

Fox Hill Farm
444 West Michigan Avenue
P.O.Box 9
Parma, MI 49269
(517) 531-3179
Fresh-cut herb plants, topiaries, ornamental and medicinal herbs.

Meadowbrook Herb Gardens
Route 138
Wyoming, RI 02898
(401) 539-7603
Organically grown herb seasonings, high quality spice and teas.

Nichols Garden Nursery
1190 N. Pacific Hwy
Albany, OR 97321
(503) 928-9280
Fresh herb plants.

Old Southwest Trading Company
P.O.Box 7545
Albuquerque, NM 87194
(800) 748-2861
(505) 831-5144

Specializes in chiles, everything from dried chiles to canned chiles and other chile-related products.

Penzey Spice House Limited
P.O. Box 1633
Milwaukee, WI 53201
(414) 768-8799
Fresh ground spices (saffron, cinnamon and peppers), bulk spices, seeds, and seasoning mixes.

Rafal Spice Company
2521 Russell Street
Detroit, MI 48207
(800) 228-4276
(313) 259-6373
Seasoning mixtures, herbs, spices, oil, coffee beans and teas.

Spice Merchant
P.O. Box 524
Jackson Hole, WY 83001
(307) 733-7811
Specializes in Asian spices.

VERMONT MAPLE SYRUP

Butternut Mountain Farm
P.O.Box 381
Johnson, VT 05656
(802) 635-7483
(800) 828-2376
Different grades of maple syrup, also a variety of honey and fruit syrups such as raspberry and blueberry.

Green Mountain Sugar House
R.F.D. #1
Ludlow, VT 05149
(802) 228-7151
(800) 647-7006
Different grades of maple syrup, maple cream and maple candies, in addition to cheese, fudge and creamed honey.

VINEGARS AND OILS

Community Kitchens
P.O. Box 2311, Dept. J-D
Baton Rouge, LA 70821-2311
(800) 535-9901
Vinegars and oil, in addition to meats, crawfish, coffees and teas.

Corti Brothers
Special gourmet items such as: imported extra-virgin olive oils, wines, exotic beans, egg pasta.
See Dried Beans and Peas

Festive Foods
Spices and herbs, teas, oils, vinegars, chocolate and baking ingredients.
See Chocolates and Candy

Kermit Lynch Wine Merchant
1605 San Pablo Ave.
Berkeley, CA 94702-1317
(510) 524-1524
(510) 528-7026 fax

Kimberly Wine Vinegar Works
290 Pierce Street
Daly City, CA 94015
(415) 755-0306
Fine wine vinegars and northern California olive oil.

Select Origins
Box N
Southampton, NY 11968
(516) 288-1382
(800) 822-2092
Oils, vinegars and rice.

Williams-Sonoma
Vinegars, oils, foods and kitchen-ware.
See Kitchen and Baking
Equipment

Conversion Index

LIQUID MEASURES

1 dash	3 to 6 drops
1 teaspoon (tsp.)	1/3 tablespoon
1 tablespoon (Tbsp.)	3 teaspoons
1 tablespoon	1/2 fluid ounce
1 fluid ounce	2 tablespoons
1 cup	1/2 pint
1 cup	16 tablespoons
1 cup	8 fluid ounces
1 pint	2 cups
1 pint	16 fluid ounces

DRY MEASURES

1 pinch	less than 1/8 teaspoon
1 teaspoon	1/3 tablespoon
1 tablespoon	3 teaspoons
1/4 cup	4 tablespoons
1/3 cup	5 tablespoons plus 1 teaspoon
1/2 cup	8 tablespoons
2/3 cup	10 tablespoons plus 2 teaspoons
3/4 cup	12 tablespoons
1 cup	16 tablespoons

VEGETABLES AND FRUITS

Apple (1 medium)	1 cup chopped
Avocado (1 medium)	1 cup mashed
Broccoli (1 stalk)	2 cups florets
Cabbage (1 large)	10 cups, chopped
Carrot (1 medium)	1/2 cup, diced
Celery (3 stalks)	1 cup, diced
Eggplant (1 medium)	4 cups, cubed
Lemon (1 medium)	2 tablespoons juice
Onion (1 medium)	1 cup diced
Orange (1 medium)	1/2 cup juice
Parsley (1 bunch)	3 cups, chopped
Spinach (fresh), 12 cups, loosely packed	1 cup cooked
Tomato (1 medium)	3/4 cup, diced
Zucchini (1 medium)	2 cups, diced

APPROXIMATE EQUIVALENTS

1 stick butter = ½ cup = 8 Tbsps. = 4 oz.
1 cup all-purpose flour = 5 oz.
1 cup cornmeal (polenta) = 4½ oz.
1 cup sugar = 8 oz.
1 cup powdered sugar = 4½ oz.
1 cup brown sugar = 6 oz.
1 large egg = 2 oz. = ¼ cup = 4 Tbsps.
1 egg yolk = 1 Tbsp. + 1 tsp.
1 egg white = 2 Tbsps. + 2 tsps.

Metric Conversions

OUNCES TO GRAMS

To convert ounces to grams, multiply number of ounces by 28.35

1 oz. ....30 g.	6 oz. ....180 g.	11 oz.......300 g.	16 oz. ......450 g.
2 oz. ....60 g.	7 oz. ....200 g.	12 oz. ......340 g.	20 oz. ......570 g.
3 oz. ....85 g.	8 oz. ....225 g.	13 oz.......370 g.	24 oz. ......680 g.
4 oz...........115 g.	9 oz. ....250 g.	14 oz. ......400 g.	28 oz. ......790 g.
5 oz. ....140 g.	10 oz. ......285 g.	15 oz. ......425 g.	32 oz. ......900 g.

QUARTS TO LITERS

To convert quarts to liters, multiply number of quarts by 0.95

1 qt. ....1 L	2½ qt........2½ L	5 qt. ....4¾ L	8 qt...........7½ L
1½ qt. ......1½ L	3 qt. ....2¾ L	6 qt...........5½ L	9 qt...........8½ L
2 qt. ....2 L	4 qt. ....3¾ L	7 qt...........6½ L	10 qt.........9½ L

FAHRENHEIT TO CELSIUS

To convert Fahrenheit to Celsius, subtract 32 from the Fahrenheit figure, multiply by 5, then divide by 9

OTHER METRIC CONVERSIONS

To convert **ounces to milliliters,** multiply number of ounces by 30

To convert **cups to liters,** multiply number of cups by 0.24

To convert **inches to centimeters,** multiply number of inches by 2.54

Recipe Index

About the Author

KATHLEEN DEVANNA FISH, author of the popular "Secrets" series, is a gourmet cook who is always on the lookout for recipes with style and character.

In addition to *New England's Cooking Secrets,* the California native has written *Cape Cod's Cooking Secrets, The Great Vegetarian Cookbook,The Great California Cookbook, California Wine Country Cooking Secrets, San Francisco's Cooking Secrets, Monterey's Cooking Secrets, New England's Cooking Secrets,* and *Cooking and Traveling Inn Style.*

Before embarking on a writing and publishing career, she owned and operated three businesses in the travel and hospitality industry.

She and her husband, Robert, live on a boat in the Monterey harbor with their black lab, Dreamer.

ROBERT FISH, award-winning photojournalist, produces the images that bring together the concept of the "Secrets" series.

In addition to taking the cover photographs, Robert explores the food and wine of each region, helping to develop the overview upon which each book is based.

Bon Vivant Press

P.O. Box 1994
Monterey, CA 93942
800-524-6826
408-373-0592
408-373-3568 FAX

Send _____ copies of *New England's Cooking Secrets* at $14.95 each.

Send _____ copies of *The Great Vegetarian Cookbook* at $14.95 each.

Send _____ copies of *The Great California Cookbook* at $14.95 each.

Send _____ copies of *California Wine Country Cooking Secrets* at $13.95 each.

Send _____ copies of *San Francisco's Cooking Secrets* at $13.95 each.

Send _____ copies of *Monterey's Cooking Secrets* at $13.95 each.

Send _____ copies of *Cape Cod's Cooking Secrets* at $14.95 each.

Add $3.00 postage and handling for the first book ordered and $1.50 for each additional book. Please add $1.08 sales tax per book, for those books shipped to California addresses.

Please charge my ☐ Visa
☐ MasterCard # _____

Expiration date_____ Signature _____

Enclosed is my check for _____

Name _____

Address_____

City_____ State_____ Zip _____

☐ This is a gift. Send directly to:

Name _____

Address_____

City_____ State_____ Zip _____

☐ Autographed by the author
Autographed to_____

NOTES